D1741778

Employment of the Month: The Unfortunately True Adventures

of

FAXBoy + FileGrrl

FBFG

NEW YORK/NOVA SCOTIA

© FAXBoy + FileGrrl 2018

All Photos by FAXBoy

Cover by Juraj Podolak

Additional Graphic Design by

Patrick Stephenson

Proofread by Ori Fienberg

employmentofthemonth.blogspot.com

License Notes and Legalese:

This book is licensed for your personal enjoyment only. If you would like to share this book with another person, please purchase an additional copy for that person. If you're reading this book and you did not purchase it, or it was not purchased for your use only, then please return to Amazon and purchase your own (damn) copy. Thank you for respecting the hard work of these authors.

Names have been changed.

ISBN: 9781730878855

Dedication

This book is dedicated to anyone who has ever had a job and lost it and to everyone who currently has a job that they no longer want.

Contents

Fast Eddie's

Employee:

FileGrrl

Location:

Loch Sheldrake, New York

Approximate Tenure:

1 1/2 weeks in the fall of 1981

Position Held:

Sandwich Maker/Cashier

AKA:

New Girl

Elapsed Time Before Job Search Resumed:

One week

Compensation:

$0.00

Commute:

A mile walk along a county highway, the pleasantness eclipsed by the ocular and bronchial onslaught of exhaust fumes from passing cars and trucks.

Commute Time:

15 - 20 minutes

Physical Environment:

A '70s deli on a beautiful lake said to contain Jimmy Hoffa's body. Very small, perhaps four tables total. Everything seemed second-hand and well used.

The meats, cheeses, and rolls were, strangely enough, very fresh and very good the first week. By the second, though, the deli case was noticeably sparse (as if someone had forgotten to place an order or was stealing slabs of roast beef. Or perhaps both).

The rumors about the deli were flying from the get-go: the store was a front and Eddie was a bookie. Eddie had mob connections. Eddie was laundering money. Eddie was this. Eddie was that. But word on the street was also that Eddie needed some help and I arrived at exactly the right time. I figured I could at least make a few sandwiches for fellow students and make some cash. Nothing else was really my business and all of it was hearsay, anyway.

I worked approximately five shifts over two weekends at minimum wage.

Emotional Environment:

It was free (as Eddie was rarely around). He made sure I could make a decent sandwich, accurately count change, and mop a floor. After that, I was completely on my own.

Nemeses:

None

Allies:

None

Living Situation(s): Alone, in a glorious if somewhat shabby, one-room bungalow. The entire area was decaying in its own pitiful way; the bars I drank in were where KISS allegedly got its start, the school the same as it was when Gene Simmons had attended at least ten years prior. (Would that I had had one quarter of Mr. Simmons' business acumen at the time.)

When I Knew:

The next bit of intrigue was that my shift partner, an older guy named Johnny, had shown up to work, trashed the deli, demanded his back pay, and beaten Eddie. Then, depending on who you talked to, Eddie: A) was in the hospital, B) locked the door, took the cash, and left town, or C) performed B after A. Regardless of these scenarios, or how they went down, I never saw Eddie again.

Departure:

Abrupt. I walked by the deli and it was closed. It never opened again. Eddie still owes me $75, but I've forgiven him. Really.

What I Think About When I Think About This Damn Job:

That this was my first job.

Old Hotel

Employee:

FileGrrl

Location:

Liberty, New York

Approximate Tenure:

One hour on December 24th, 1981

Position Held:

A Something

AKA:

HR Mirage

Elapsed Time Before Job Search Resumed:

Didn't stay/didn't look

Compensation:

I got to spend the holidays with my family

Commute:

Up the long driveway from employee housing to The Old Hotel, herself, through piles of snow. (And back down again.) Once. Each way.

Commute Time:

0 hours, 0 minutes, and 0 seconds (give or take a few minutes for the snow).

Physical Environment:

A freezing cold, drafty, older-than-fuck, Jewish resort in The Catskills. I parked in the semi-frozen mud in the back of something called "The Playhouse" (all slaves and *goyim* were required to slink in through the rear entrance), reported to my room, unlocked the door, flipped on the light, and found an elderly woman lying naked on her bed. She was apparently my new roommate. Neither of us had been expecting the other and she was unclothed because the ancient radiators had been cranked to full blast (as the hotel boilers were working overtime due to the weather) and they were leaking puddles of skanky, steamy sludge both onto, and into, the linoleum tiles. She'd thrown open her/our sash to let the snow in and I stepped over a small drift to get to the bathroom. I tried to make nice with her, but she wouldn't speak to me. She stood up violently to snap off the light (momentarily flashing her angry geriatric beaver at me), whipped a sheet over her shriveled body, and flopped back down on the bed with her face to the wall.

Emotional Environment:

An antique jail cell (my infraction unknown) complete with an equally-antiquated cellmate totally removed from my friends and family, from any hope of a decent meal, jokes, laughter, or privacy.

Nemeses:

My cellmate

Allies:

My '73 sun-bleached avocado Nova out in the parking lot (still warm from my commute)

Living Situation(s):

I was transitioning from one crummy apartment that I couldn't afford to another crummy apartment that I also could not afford. I loved living away from home and was looking forward to all of the new people I'd meet. I thought I'd just make new friends all the time out in the world, like we did in college and that everyone else was as eager to let the good times roll as I was. This was my introduction to the fact that everybody went home for Christmas break. No one stayed. The talk on campus was that if you landed a seasonal hotel gig, you'd work your hours and then have plenty of time to frolic or what-have-you after your shift. It was clear from the moment that I arrived, however, that this proverbial "frolicking" was not going to be part of my particular seasonal hotel-gig experience. The kids that I saw in the hallway of The Playhouse already seemed to know each other, so I was the odd woman out from the start (and I knew that this was not going to work out for me on any level, whatsoever).

When I Knew:

Strangely enough, it was a (relatively) slow burn. I took a shower to think about it. I really had my sights set on responsibility and stoicism. By the end of the shower, though, I was clean, my head was clear, and my bag was still packed.

Departure: Abrupt. I spent about twenty minutes locked in the bathroom figuring out my next move before loading everything back into the car for the two-hour drive to my parents' house through the blizzard and the blinding snow (to surprise my mom for Christmas-Eve dinner). Did not stop, did not pass "Go."

What I Think About When I Think About This Damn Job:

That naked still happens at 75. (God bless her.)

Hotel de Vile

Employee:

FileGrrl

Location:

Liberty, New York

Approximate Tenure:

Passover 1983

Position Held:

Spa Attendant

AKA:

Bathroom Maid-in-Waiting

Elapsed Time Before Job Search Resumed:

Search resumed immediately

Compensation:

Unknown ($3.50/hour, perhaps?)

Commute:

Involved listening to a lot of Led Zeppelin in the same four-wheeled faded beauty that got me to the last hotel job (until the stereo quit)

Commute Time:

One half-hour, each way (parking for sub-humans in the back, as usual)

Physical Environment:

Another nice Jewish resort. Old, venerated, established, and decrepit. The answer to every decorating conundrum and storage snafu was to drape some white-painted lattice fencing around the visual offense. (Lattice fence used indoors was Jewish resort code for "You Don't See This.") Example: A piano, covered in dust and *schmutz* with keys sorely in need of replacement, that has been wheeled out of a nightclub and into a hallway to protect its finish ("Still good!") Solution: Surround it with three large sheets of white latticework fencing, *et viola*! "You don't see it!" I caught on quick, but really, the whole place was a curiosity.

Emotional Environment:

Some combination of repressive, boring, and very depressing (which, I guess, made it "brery drepressing"). My time was spent mopping the ladies' locker room and showers. I'd grown up in a family that could easily afford to stay in better hotels, so I wasn't used to being on the other side of the housekeeping equation. It seemed an easy tit-for-tat: Do what you were asked and get a paycheck at the end of the week. But this world didn't work like that. I did what I was told, which didn't seem like very much, and I finished my assigned tasks inside of about ninety minutes. (As far as I was concerned, my work was done.) My shift was 7.5 hours long. *Then what?* There was nowhere to actually stand and nothing actually to do. Nasty Nancy, my boss and ring leader for the ladies' spa, introduced me to the idea of "work for the sake of appearances." She referred to me as The Spa Girl and in this hotel, apparently, there should always be some woman (me) scurrying to tidy up after guests. I should be fastidious about tidiness. (I wasn't all that concerned.) Once a wastebasket was emptied, it was empty, and I could not improve upon its emptiness. I'd no idea how to play concierge to people who wouldn't talk to me. What I mistook for rudeness was really symptomatic of the social pecking order. As soon as I understood that part, I just checked out emotionally. From their standpoint, I'm certain that I was viewed as the laziest Spa Girl in the world.

Nemeses:

Nasty Nancy, Spa Hostess. She was a fixture with her own podium and appointment book and she *loved* to order me around. I don't think it was personal; it's just what she did with all of her underlings. She didn't want me to waste a single second. The problem being, there really wasn't that much to do, other than to pick up towels, wheel them to the laundry facility at the other end of the hotel, pour orange juice into little pleated paper cups, and arrange them on the dark brown plastic trays perched on the edge of the hot tub. By day three, I wised up considerably and tucked *The Lord of the Rings* into my pants. When my work was caught up and Nasty Nancy wasn't looking, I'd slip into a vacant toilet stall, shut the door, pull my feet up, sit on the back of one of the johns, and catch up with Frodo and Bilbo. I could kill a good 45 minutes this way. I knew I wouldn't last long and I really didn't care.

Allies:

J.R.R. Tolkien

Living Situation(s):

My own student "apartment," *sans* roommate. Heaven on Earth. "Apartment" meaning: two small bedrooms, a crappy kitchen, and a bathroom. No living space beyond the mattress on the floor and the dresser, but at least I had privacy. My roommate was absent (mostly) because she was *very* busy snorting cocaine all across Iceland on holiday, but I remember that she did manage to bring me back a nice sweater.

When I Knew:

When some Pretty Young Thing looked me dead in the eye and dropped her towel at my feet. I can venture to say that nearly every woman who went to the spa was, in fact, evil incarnate. If I cared, I'd have had to kill someone. It was easier to keep a game face on, to silently pick up after the nasty bitches, and not to give in.

Departure:

The end of Passover. (Thank baby Jesus...)

What I Think About When I Think About This Damn Job: White fluffy towels. Toilets. Hobbits. Ladies with lots and lots of gold jewelry and fur coats, but no personality whatsoever. Nazgûls. Lonely little lunches, of matzoh wafers with butter or chicken soup with matzoh, in the low-ceilinged employee dining hall. Loneliness (because I was the only person in the room who spoke English as a first language). Being reprimanded for drinking one of the tiny cups filled with forbidden orange juice, as they so obviously were not for me, which easily made it the tastiest (canned) OJ I've ever had. Being called a "towel bimmy," the exact meaning of which I've never quite figured out, but whose vaguely derogatory nature was not lost on me.

Cajün Bürger Führer

Employee:

FileGrrl

Location:

Houma, Louisiana

Approximate Tenure:

Two months during the sweltering summer of 1985

Position Held:

Lunchtime Drive-Thru Specialist/Dishwasher

AKA:

Dumb Yankee

Elapsed Time Before Job Search Resumed:

I didn't look because I knew that I'd be escaping back to school in the fall.

Compensation:

As little as legally possible

Commute:

Sprint from my parents' air-conditioned apartment into my mom's third (and also air-conditioned) Buick Regal. Dodge dead armadillos on the highway, drop mom off at her job, and then take my life into my own hands through the super-scariest intersection in town to run back into the air conditioning (and bürger glory) of *Le Führer*.

Commute Time:

20 minutes

Physical Environment:

Well, you know.

Emotional Environment:

Fascinating. I was on the outside looking in 110% of the time. I would wash dishes until I got called to the drive-thru window for the noon rush and then report back to dish duty and a shift supervisor who didn't speak any English whatsoever. Her sentences were a blaze of French, Spanish, and Something that I could never make out. I'd just left a semester's worth of schoolgirl, introductory French, yet couldn't even grab a stray <<*Je*>> from the air. Everyone spoke this machine-gun dialect. Except me. The random assortment of people who worked at *Le Führer* would often start their conversations in English. They'd wax on about going to church, what to wear to church, and who they'd seen at church and then, in the next sentence, they'd start talking about how fucked up they'd been on Friday night. ("Oh, girrrrrrrl, I was sooooo fuuucked uuuup! Momma don' knooow!!") After these intriguing introductions, they'd inevitably leave me in the linguistic dust and I'd be left to fill in the particulars with my own (monolingual) imagination. The Friday-night-hooch-absolved-by-the-Sunday-go-to-meetin's went on all summer long.

Nemeses:

None. (Well, maybe the Fry-O-Lator or the Dish-A-Doer...)

Allies:

None of these, either. My shift supervisor did seem to pity me (in her own way), perhaps because I was ignorant and from up North. Sometimes she'd remind the others to speak English around me, but any personal business was conducted in the rapid-fire tongue that was romantic to hear, but depressingly exclusionary. I brought a book to read by myself (written in English) on day three.

Living Situation(s):

I was staying with my mom and my stepfather. I lived in my sister's room and taped pictures of my friends from back home to the walls just to remind myself that I actually did have friends. Somewhere.

When I Knew:

I always knew.

Departure:

I left appropriately. My stepfather had used some sort of connection to get me into *Le Führer* and I was too scared to ruin that relationship. I was representing for The North as best I could and didn't want to be a social ingrate by messing up a flippin' burger job. I had no place else to go as I was, almost literally, a prisoner of the heat, the swamp, the bugs, the snakes, and the spiders. Autumn was my escape clause.

What I Think About When I Think About This Damn Job:

I think of my fantasies of New Orleans, of being trapped, and of finally understanding that I needed to help my family out with money. Finding out on the phone from Madame that I'd passed textbook French back in New York and then bursting into tears because I couldn't understand one fucking word of the crazy spoken French that I heard six hours a day, eight days a week, down on the bayou.

The Department of Parks and Wreckreation

Employee:

FAXBoy

Location:

Litigation City, New York

Approximate Tenure:

The summers of 1986 and 1987

Position Held:

Seasonal Employee

AKA:

LawnBoy

Elapsed Time Before Job Search Resumed:

I liked driving the tractor, so how was I to know that there might be something better out there?

Compensation:

$4.1229389438211/hour (with unlimited free tanning)

Commute:

A quick walk from the foster home to Smithfield Park

Commute Time:

Five minutes(-ish)

Physical Environment:

For two summers in high school, I lived in a big corrugated-steel garage from Monday to Friday with two old men who had been working together since before parks were invented.

They resembled Laurel and Hardy from a TV show that was taped just after television was invented (one guy had a big belly and a bit of an attitude and the other guy was a skinny [but loveable!] drunk with a couple of front teeth missing). When it rained, we could spend the whole day inside the enormous, glorified tool shed with the aforementioned tractor, assorted push mowers, weed-whackers, Rototillers, rakes, shovels, and ice picks (not so useful in the summer, by the way...) Laurel and Hardy loved to play cards and even though I don't (at all), I liked hanging out and being away from the foster home for extended periods of time.

Emotional Environment:

Like being babysat by intoxicated uncles who make you do chores while you're with them.

Nemeses:

Wasps and hornets

Allies:

Laurel and Hardy

Living Situation(s):

Plantation-style foster home with two gender-appropriate overseers and another foster kid.

When I Knew:

I didn't, actually. (Have I mentioned how much fun it was to drive the tractor?)

Departure:

After two summers, I was reassigned to another city job by one of the politically-connected overseers.

What I Think About When I Think About This Damn Job:

The sun. Grinding the soil around the baseball field with a massive, diesel-powered, shiny red machine. The smell of gasoline and fresh-cut grass. The sensational combination of earning money without carrying any debt. The James-Dean-esque allure of smoking. That I wish that every subsequent job had had such an amazing lack of supervision as this first one.

Barker's Discount

Employee:

FileGrrl

Location:

Somewhere, New York

Approximate Tenure:

One week in the fall of 1987

Position Held:

Sales Associate

AKA:

Gun Bitch

Elapsed Time Before Job Search Resumed:

One week

Compensation:

$4.65/hour (or thereabouts)

Commute:

A short drive through beautiful downtown Somewhere in a green machine, which means that it might have been the beat-up Chevy Nova, but that it could also have been a rusted Ford of unknown provenance.

Commute Time:

15 minutes, each way

Physical Environment:

Pleasant if you like wearing an orange smock and being surrounded by screaming juice-stained infants and distraught Upstate New York moms.

Emotional Environment:

I'm pretty sure that management was convinced that I was mentally challenged.

Nemeses:

The Clock

Allies:

None

Living Situation(s):

In a large, inelegant apartment house with a revolving door of people (some friends, some enemies). It was often difficult to keep track of who was which on any given day.

When I Knew:

The day that management transferred me from the ladies' clothing department to guns and autos. Male customers would deride me for not knowing the difference between one shotgun shell and another and for not being able to assist them with any of the lubricants, oils, tires, or waxing agents. (And I didn't blame them one bit.)

Departure:

Abrupt. Took phone off hook. Burned smock.

What I Think About When I Think About This Damn Job:

The smell of stale popcorn from the machine in the lobby. The turquoise-and-orange décor. Blasting Joy Division in the car with Joe at the end of each shift (and listening to him read excerpts from whatever book he was immersed in at the time) to detox me back to reality. (Or perhaps, out of reality.)

The Kamikaze Clothing Company

Employee:

FileGrrl

Location:

Somewhere, New York

Approximate Tenure:

Two weeks in the spring of 1988

Position Held:

Stitcher

AKA:

That Slow Girl

Elapsed Time Before Job Search Resumed:

Two weeks

Compensation:

Piece Work (about 10¢, 25¢, or 80¢ per sleeve set, back flap, or zipper closure)

Commute:

Another short drive through Somewhere to a parking lot surrounded by a fence laced with barbed wire. (I could never figure out if the barbed wire was to keep us in, tethered to our machines, or to keep outsiders from suddenly clawing their way onto the factory floor.)

After searching for a space in the lot, I'd enter the factory and immediately don my blue smock. Then I'd run past two hundred other women wearing blue smocks all doing calisthenics. I was late for calisthenics nearly every morning (as the General Tojo routine required me to arrive a full ten minutes before my shift actually started). Only once or twice did I make it to my workstation on time for the workout broadcast. I liked doing jumping jacks in my blue smock to some extent (it fell into some neo-Orwellian activity for me that was interesting from a purely observational standpoint).

Commute Time:

10 minutes

Physical Environment:

A stadium-sized factory cranking out swanky Japanese designer coats and jackets ready to be trucked down to Manhattan. Patriarchal, like The Imperial Army: The battalions of women in the aforementioned blue smocks were overseen by male commanding officers wearing white-collared shirts.

Emotional Environment:

Owned. From the moment we sat down after jumping jacks to the moment the bell rang at the end of the day, we were owned. Nevertheless, we were done with work by 3PM or so, at which point I'd crawl back to bed.

Nemeses:

Self: I got the job because I could sew a fairly fast, straight seam and hit all the marks on the pre-fab test strips done on their huge industrial units. I'd never seen a clutch-machine before, much less operated one, but my tests were good enough for me to land the job. However, I slowed down as I became introspective and depressed. My stitches were still perfect, but I executed them in a slow, obsessive sort of way, not a speedy can't-wait-to-get-a-paycheck kind of way. Getting up at 6AM did not help one bit. I was at the top end of a fantastic summer, attempting to balance a wild-in-the-streets nightlife with a soar-with-the-eagles, crack-of-bleeding-dawn factory job and, as a result, my body shut down with bronchitis by week two. The shop foreman believed in me and kept moving me from machine to machine, and from station to station, in the hopes that I'd find something that I clicked with (to finally become useful). But really, I like to sew, but not rivet or punch. I did my duty and took my turn at various machines, never really allowed to get the hang of any of them before they switched my station once again. On my last day, the foreman came around and tossed me into a room with a group of Pakistani and Asian hand-stitchers. In a mixture of American Sign Language, Urdu, and Korean, they showed me how to loop the thread to make a quick knot, how the stitches should be wrapped, clean and hidden. I was way out of my league.

Allies:

The Indian lady who brought home remedies for my cough: slices of freeze-dried ginger wrapped in aluminum foil and soup that tasted of curry, carrots, and socks.

Living Situation(s):

Transitional. I had a small apartment in reserve, but needed to wait three weeks to move in. I lived alternately in my car and on my friend, Mary's, sofa. Mary insisted that I sleep in her antique four-poster bed with her aging Siamese (who drooled). I'm not sure where Mary slept. I left for work so early in the morning that I think we may have been sharing the bed, and the aging cat, in shifts.

When I Knew:

As a newly minted art-school graduate, I was delusional. I thought I would work my way up through the ranks to the design office, learning all of the processes along the way, until finally, because of my diligence and obvious spunk, I would be presented with a drafting table and a set of pencils with which to create fashion-forward rainwear for the developing world. When they started switching me from machine to machine, I knew that I was being groomed for greatness.

Departure:

Abrupt. I was ushered into a room and told that I was too slow and that I didn't "fit in." Have a nice life. I burst into tears.

What I Think About When I Think About This Damn Job:

That this was my first job after college. That the foreman had just purchased my stepfather's house on Muckity Muck Drive and that I don't think that he really understood exactly why I was working in his factory. That I hadn't spoken to my stepparents in nearly two years and, as a woman on the move, I needed the money.

Daybreakery

Employee:

FileGrrl

Location:

Somewhere, New York

Approximate Tenure:

Two weeks in the summer of 1988

Position Held:

Bakery Help

AKA:

Bakery Bitch

Elapsed Time Before Job Search Resumed:

Two months. I don't remember leaving. I just know it was a long time before I worked again.

Compensation:

$6.00/hour

Commute:

A futile sprint to the bakery to unlock the door (late) and then re-lock it behind me. Another sprint to the back of the bakery to pull on a filthy apron and to fire up the oven (if the mother-in-law had not arrived and started it already). I'd turn on the giant, stainless-steel mixer; add flour, sugar, yeast, water, and then proof for three hours as the whole mixture died a slow death in the warmer. In my defense, the recipe for this large batch of rolls was hand-written by the aforementioned mother-in-law on several sheets of notebook paper in which the ink had smeared from the pages due to the amount of water that sprayed all over *everything* constantly. Sometimes it felt like we worked directly underneath Niagara Falls.

Commute Time:

10 minutes

Physical Environment:

The kitchen of a local bakery that I'd remembered from when I was a kid (except that now my former philosophy professor had taken ownership and was trying to make a go of it).

It was completely old school (even while I was growing up), and I think it was a dull grey on the outside, but the inside was full of marvelous treats. I used to cut class in high school, fill a bag to bursting (if I happened to have the money), and spend the afternoon in the park with a book and a slew of pastries.

Emotional Environment:

Oppressive and failure-inducing with tons of physical labor and dishwashing and all of the introspection that comes with that. My former philosophy professor ran it with his wife, who simply hated me, and his mother-in-law who was kinder, but equally terrifying. The kitchen was large and professional, but there were only three of us. We worked our tails off non-stop to produce fresh rolls, breads, cookies, and lunch sandwiches.

Time until inevitable death of our daily bread: three hours.

Nemeses:

My philosophy teacher's wife and his mother-in-law. But especially his wife who seemed to be overtly threatened by me sexually, even though I must have been absolutely ravishing in my sweatpants and dirty apron. (I had no interest in her husband, whatsoever. Less than that, even.)

Allies:

Strangely enough, my philosophy teacher.

I think he felt sorry for me as he made several faint attempts to justify the totally flattened dough, which only made his wife increase the frequency of her quiet insults to my intelligence and general worth as a bread baker (and as a human being). She enjoyed emotionally destroying him, as well, and I once embarrassed the two of them by catching them arguing over my future in the kitchen. Seeing her in action went a long way toward explaining his basic hang-dog appearance during his night classes, and I spent much of my time as a baker and as a dishwasher wondering how someone smart enough to understand Immanuel Kant could have married someone so stupid and so mean. I also went out on my own existential limb thinking that a professor of philosophy should never have to perform manual labor in a family-owned bakery. At the time, I lived in a world of romantic stereotypes where philosophy teachers were allowed to do nothing more than wear black turtlenecks, teach classes, conduct research, and write incredibly convoluted sentences for articles published in scholarly journals using only the most obscure polysyllabic words that the English language had to offer. Observing him with her at the bakery was like learning that the king of a country actually had to milk his own cows. The feedback loop to this was incredible. I'm not sure I ever got over it, although I did learn to block it out.

Living Situation(s):

In a rooming house with three Narcotics Anonymous members who helped to care for a raving, yet still-engaged, alcoholic emeritus history professor. When I moved in, I thought that I had rented a nice room in an old house that just happened to have a nice old man living downstairs.

I was wrong.

One of the NA members was a biker, named Savage, and we took turns keeping the house in livable order. (Otherwise, it would have sunk to some pretty low depths.) I made a promise to myself then never to live with drug addicts again, even by accident. My room was quite nice, though, as it was once the master bedroom. I painted it ivory to cover up the pea-green walls, hung some lace curtains and a somber band poster that had been a gift from a man. I had a lock on my door, so while addictions and bikers might rage all around me, I inhabited a peaceful haven.

When I Knew:

The third day in a row that my philosophy teacher's mother-in-law bustled into the kitchen, her perfume wafting into the yeast-laden breeze, to poo-poo the deceased dinner rolls and to inform me that I had no business *being* in a kitchen. I am a fairly substantial cook, but at the time, I had no business in a kitchen, that I cannot deny.

Departure:

No recollection. I think I just didn't show up one day. I might have been in the hospital…

What I Think About When I Think About This Damn Job:

The bulimic who came in, ordered two lunch platters and every dessert on the menu, ate it all by herself, and then scurried into the ladies' room. Halston perfume. (In fact, every time I get a rare whiff of the stuff, I'm transported to a rather dark time and place that makes *me* want to throw up.)

The Mailroom in The Crapitol

Employee:

FAXBoy

Location:

Litigation City, New York

Approximate Tenure:

The summer of 1988

Position Held:

Seasonal Employee

AKA:

MailBoy

Elapsed Time Before Job Search Resumed:

This was the summer before my freshman year in The Ivy League, so I wasn't thinking too much past getting the hell out of Litigation City

Compensation:

$4.219234871928374/hour

Commute:

A brisk walk straight "downtown" from the foster home to the small cluster of extremely boring government buildings huddled around an emotionally-distant government plaza.

Commute Time:

15 minutes(-ish)

Physical Environment:

The mailroom was buried deep within the bowels of the enormous Crapitol building and was proportionally enormous, as well. There were stacks and stacks of yellow, yellowed, and yellowing papers, phone books, take-out menus, and not-so-clandestine porno mags in wire baskets on a half-dozen surplus metal desks from the 50s manned (as there were no women when I worked there) by a few surplus men in their 50s (who wouldn't leave until after they retired) and a few men in their 20s (who never wanted to be there in the first place).

Emotional Environment:

Was kinda fun, like detention for forty hours a week, but with music.

Nemeses:

Politicians, lawyers, and their respective staff members. (Basically, anyone that I delivered mail to.)

Allies:

The Heavy Metal Mailman and The Really Drunk Guy

Living Situation(s):

The aforementioned plantation-style foster home with two gender-appropriate overseers and another foster kid.

When I Knew:

Again, I didn't. (Really.) I was counting the minutes until I went off to college, so I was just psyched to be making some cash before I blew this particular Popsicle stand, never to look back.

Departure:

Official (officially), yet drunken (unofficially). I finished out the summer, but got drunk with The Really Drunk Guy in an official New York State vehicle in the parking lot underneath the stately behemoth. The Really Drunk Guy insisted that I go out to lunch with him and lunch consisted of two six-packs of Budweiser and a pack of Kools. We spent the afternoon of my last day sorting and delivering very official, and very important, mail in a cheap domestic haze.

What I Think About When I Think About This Damn Job:

The incredibly loud machine that metered the mail. It was like a giant bronze and pewter animal from the turn of the last century that somehow calculated and attached the correct postage to all of the outgoing correspondence that it ate and shit out (simultaneously, at break-neck speeds). The fluorescent light fixtures that hung low from the ceiling that looked like those old-school metal ice cube trays (the ones that had the lever that looked like a hand brake running down the middle of them). Writing the chorus to The Heavy Metal Mailman's one and only hit, "Hangin' and Bangin'," in about thirty seconds after I got tired of him trying to sound it out over the course of a very long week. Reading the review about the chorus in *Metroland* after their next show and feeling proud of my heavy-metal handiwork.

Sage Dining Hall

Employee:

FAXBoy

Location:

Ivy League, New York

Approximate Tenure:

My freshman year in college, from 1988-1989

Position Held:

Generic Student Kitchen Help

AKA:

The New Guy

Elapsed Time Before Job Search Resumed:

I didn't even think about another job while I had this one because I got a discount on my meal plan and free food while I was on the clock.

Compensation:

$3.50(-ish)/hour (It weren't much, I can tell you that much.)

Commute:

Three blocks on foot

Commute Time:

Four minutes in the fall and spring. 10-to-15 in the winter.

Physical Environment:

Like a moldy basement in an old, brick mansion.

Emotional Environment:

Detention-esque, but not *so* bad

Nemeses:

Kafka and students without jobs

Allies:

Everyone I worked with (can you imagine?)

Living Situation(s):

In a dorm, I mean "residence hall," down by the crick.

When I Knew:

I didn't. I was greener than green.

Departure:

Official with all of the other student employees at the end of the spring semester. Everyone was all smiles and "Have a great summer!" at each other. I don't think that these types of congenial work environments exist anymore in America.

What I Think About When I Think About This Damn Job:

Dumping hot soup directly into my boss's shoes on the first day(!) No lie. I was working on the line, I turned to grab a stainless-steel bucket of minestrone from the kitchen behind me, secured it with a couple of asbestos mitts, turned back towards the steam table in front of me, hit him vaguely hip-range, and poured the molten vegetable goodness right down his legs and into his shoes. There was no skin lost, no emergency medical treatment (that I can remember), but I was MORTIFIED and overly-apologetic for the rest of the lunch shift.

The old, mottled, and very thin carpeting laid over the bumpy concrete floor in the dining room. Being responsible for maintaining the dairy station one day, opening the massive door to the milk dispenser, and being confronted with a massive cockroach splayed out (and defying gravity) on the side of the 2% container. Grabbing the rag from my back pocket and using it to apprehend the beast and then, feeling like I had Gregor Samsa squirming in my pocket, carrying the fortunate thing all the way out the back door before releasing it/him back into the wild.

Fabric Store #1

Employee:

FileGrrl

Location:

Somewhere, New York

Approximate Tenure:

One month during the spring of 1989

Position Held:

Clerk

AKA:

Mind Reader

Elapsed Time Before Job Search Resumed:

One week

Compensation:

No recollection. $4.00/hour? (Completely unremarkable.)

Commute:

A brisk walk with the same dread in the pit of my stomach every day knowing that no matter what I did, everything would still be utterly wrong when I arrived.

Commute Time:

10 Minutes

Physical Environment:

Small, privately rented shop that sold fabric to art students, ladies who sewed, and quilters.

Emotional Environment:

Damned. Just damned.

Nemeses:

Store owner and overseer

Allies:

None

Living Situation(s):

With Meekon and The Merry Drunksters. I, however, was not drunk. Nor was I using, but everyone else in the house seemed to be. Except for Savage, who looked like he was both drunk and using, but wasn't.

When I Knew:

When a package arrived for my boss, in a large box, during his lunch hour, and I happily signed for it and placed it on the counter so that he would see it when he walked into the store. He came back with his lunch, ate about half of it, and sent me on break (and to be honest, a break was my only opportunity to breathe, the tension was so incredibly thick when this guy was around). When I walked back in after exhaling, I could sense that I was in trouble for some infraction of his unwritten rules. Again. "When were you going to tell me I'd received this package?" "Um, I thought you'd just see it and open it." (I am personally always so gleeful about correspondence of any sort that I even open my junk mail, so it never occurred to me that a grown man wouldn't see a large cardboard box sitting on the counter of his own business.) The passive aggression was fascinating only from a distance. He told me that a competent, professional, store clerk would be able to alert her boss to the arrival of such packages and that I should let him know *immediately* when *anything* was delivered. Well, at least that rule was clear! (Except that there were many more, stated and unstated, where that one came from.) The second time (in one week!) that he kept me after-hours counting the drawer down for the sixth time because it was a single goddamn penny off, I just knew. In fact, I spent quite a bit of time in the shop wondering how his wife could have stayed married to him long enough to produce the amazing child-spawn who would grow up to be classmates with my brother. His arbitrary strictness was such a puzzle.

Departure:

I called out with the flu (which, in fact, I had pretty badly as I was so incredibly stressed out from this fabric shop and The Merry Drunksters screaming at each other over mountains of cocaine every night). The following week, when I went in to pick up my paycheck (a dreaded chore I needed to mentally prepare for), he fired me on the spot. Case closed. Thank god.

What I Think About When I Think About This Damn Job: Meekon and The Merry Drunksters. (I wonder if they ever got clean and sober at the NA meetings they were all going to?) That guy who shot himself down the street and the cleaning crew that was brought in to mop him off of the porch and how this bothered me for months. Having the flu in late winter while my lover took some other girl to The Bahamas and, upon returning, left pictures of her (in a skimpy blue bikini draped across the bed of their cabana with gorgeous palm trees swaying in the background) on his coffee table when I came over (as if he was trying to end our relationship with a sort of industrial-strength nonchalance). How this was my last job in this city.

That Plumbing Supply Place

Employee:

FileGrrl

Location:

Albany, New York

Approximate Tenure:

One day in April of 1989

Position Held:

Temporary Administrative Assistant

AKA:

Sick

Elapsed Time Before Job Search Resumed:

Four Hours

Compensation:

$5.00/hour

Commute:

The Crapital District Transit Authority's # 55 (that smelly, smoke-infused, angry-ghetto-chic-haulin', brawl-inducing caravan of a bus). Crap, how I hate that line.

Commute Time:

30 – 42 minutes for what was otherwise a 10-minute trip

Physical Environment:

A plumbing showroom in a derelict brick warehouse which may have been a garage back in the 1950s. My desk was kitty corner to the actual corner of the large room, filled with fixtures and piping, toilets, stalls and posters. My window was a garage door to my left. The best part was the wall calendar of *Playboy* Bunnies hung on a nail directly behind me. I really knew my place. I'd been prepped that the company was having a hard time holding onto temps.

Emotional Environment:

Oppressive. I was instructed to type client letters on a manual typewriter and there was no Wite-Out® in sight. They'd never heard of a word processor, much less a computer with WordPerfect® (which was the standard at the time). I pecked all morning long, mistake after mistake.

Nemeses:

The manual typewriter. (See above.)

Allies:

None

Living Situation(s):

With John, who hated me. John had a poster of Bob Seger and The Silver Bullet Band on the wall in the living room, so I really should have known that we'd have nothing in common.

When I Knew:

The minute I walked in and saw the girlie calendar.

Something about that just threw me. I don't mind girls or calendars, but in the context of a work environment that required me to type 40 – 50WPM, The Bunnies were really odd. Now I think I'd just recycle it and not say a word. They were so insistent about my so-called "professionalism," yet the environment set women back at least forty years.

Departure:

Ah-choo, motherfuckers! I made up a cold at lunch hour and called out the next day. I was informed that I was the last temp the company was going to hire, as temps just weren't working out there. (Perhaps Hugh Heffner could send someone over on a more permanent basis? Maybe she could bring her own computer and printer?)

What I Think About When I Think About This Damn Job:

I think of St. Pauli Girls and *Playboy* and the days of the week. Girls in Santa outfits, girls in fishnets and heels, girls with fake boobs. Girls! Girls! Girls!

The Department of Fiscal Difficulties

Employee:

FAXBoy

Location:

Litigation City, New York

Approximate Tenure:

The summer of 1989

Position Held:

Seasonal Employee

AKA:

Unwanted Trainee For Nonexistent Job

Elapsed Time Before Job Search Resumed:

In a bizarre turn of events, I asked (emphatically) to keep this job at the end of the summer.

Compensation:

$4.310293805293840349/hour

Commute:

Five or six blocks straight "downtown" from my first apartment to the same group of government buildings on the same government plaza as my mailroom gig to The Jones Building (across the park from The Crapitol Building).

Commute Time:

Five minutes(-ish)

Physical Environment:

State office that took up the entire fluorescently-lit floor of The Jones Building that could have done double duty as the set of a hard-boiled 70s cop show, shot in New York City, by a wildly unsteady cameraman.

Emotional Environment:

Like spending forty (or rather, 37.654 repeating) hours in a standardized-testing facility. I felt like I had to perform to the best of my abilities at all times even though I didn't necessarily understand the questions.

Nemeses:

The clock. The foster people.

Allies:

Kaitlyn, my immediate boss (and one of the perkiest, tightestly-curled, blond women I have ever met).

Living Situation(s):

A room in a three-(or four-)bedroom apartment in a big brick apartment building on Willet Street with my friend, Natasha, and her stoner friends. I had a mattress on the floor, a beat-up stereo that somebody gave to me, and my bag of paints and brushes. The apartment had a great living room and a huge kitchen, but it was a little like living in a gigantic bong because the place always smelled like weed.

When I Knew:

Things had gone sufficiently south in the foster home that I really needed to keep this job at the time but they, unfortunately, couldn't keep me.

Departure:

Strange and awkward, but official.

What I Think About When I Think About This Damn Job:

How happy I was to get out of the foster house (if only for a summer). Unexpected sex with Natasha. Getting some of my poems published for the first time. Being taught to program, loving computers and technology, and realizing later that this may have been the last time that I actually learned anything on the job.

Lemme's Market

Employee:

FileGrrl

Location:

Albany, New York

Approximate Tenure:

No recollection (Late 80s? Early 90s? It's a blur…)

Position Held:

Cashier

AKA:

New Girl

Elapsed Time Before Job Search Resumed:

Several months

Compensation:

An hourly wage that averaged out somewhere in the six figures, no doubt.

Commute:

I walked across Washington Park to the hip side of town. (Back when the town had a "hip" side.)

Commute Time:

20 - 25 minutes

Physical Environment:

Crumbling bodega. Two dirty, 19th-century residential buildings had been cobbled together on Lark Street into a very strange makeshift grocery mess. There were two or three kitchens on premises to make the "home-made" goods. Made fresh, the food was very good, in spite of the creature problems. The floors were decayed linoleum tile, with high-traffic areas worn through to whatever made up the next layer. The walls were painted (and repainted) bead board; the staircase was shaky, narrow, and dark. Ooo, how I loved it here!

Emotional Environment:

Festive (in a down-and-on-our-way-out sort of way).

Nemeses:

None

Allies:

The owner, Georgio, who must have inherited this masterpiece of a storefront from a family member. As hard as he worked to maintain suppliers and inspections, I think that he understood the extent to which it was a lost cause. Paul. Paul was the quintessential Goth guy. He dressed in late 18th-century garb every day. *Every* day. He, admittedly, took over an hour to get ready in the morning and it showed from the tip of his wiry ponytail (tied with a black bow) to the edges of his frock coat, garters, and stockings. When I started this gig, I had the feeling that I was going to find a kindred spirit in Paul.

We used to take lunch together on the dark staircase that led to the second kitchen to discuss how weird it was working for this grocery store at this time in history, the oddness of the drunk patrons, the junkies, the drag queens, the old, phlegmatic men, the occasional super-hot chic, and so on. (*"Why us? Why now? Why Lemme's?"*) In any case, he invited me to his apartment to meet the girlfriend (an angry Russian who wore late 19th-century corsets, petticoats, and black eyeliner), and my hunch had been right: I loved hanging out with Paul and Mina. I loved their apartment, their moods, their music, and their general dissatisfaction. They were Royalists in a country that has never had a queen.

Living Situation(s):

I lived with crew members from the local university. They got up every day before dawn to best the river and returned each morning exhausted and slept until noon. They were fairly miserable to live with, but experimental. One hated me and my quiet, well-behaved cat, and when he was sober, he'd blast Pat Metheny until I needed to cry or leave the building and the other guy eventually gave up sculling and the river to grow dreads and skunk weed in his closet.

The skunk took over the living space as only skunk can, and suddenly it was skunk "season" and we had visitors day and night, "friends" who would "drop by" for dime bags at all hours. At some point, a motorcycle became a permanent installation in our living room. (There were newspapers underneath it to catch the oil, at least.)

Skinheads arrived and waited for meals. Someone walked into our kitchen late one night to rifle through my purse, but all they got was my last five bucks and a pack of clove cigarettes.

I moved out in the fall.

When I Knew:

I always knew this wouldn't last forever. I suppose I found something more respectable that allowed me to leave the three part-time jobs I was holding at the time just to make my rent.

Departure:

An actual, official, two-week notice to the owner.

What I Think About When I Think About This Damn Job:

The guy who walked in and bought a scratch-off ticket from me and won, then used the winnings to buy five more and won on those, and ended up buying nearly thirty scratch-offs and walking out of the store over $200 up. The small crowd that gathered around us to cheer him on. In some twilight recess, I think I always believed that it would last: the people, the sales of lemons and limes to the local bartenders heading into their shifts, the conversations with the beautiful man on the stairs, the idea that I could earn a few honest dollars before disappearing into my own black-clad evenings...

Regional Puppet Fuckers

Employee:

FileGrrl

Location:

Troy, New York

Approximate Tenure:

One afternoon in the fall of 1991

Position Held:

Costume Designer

AKA:

Stupid

Elapsed Time Before Job Search Resumed:

One week – I actually didn't know that they didn't need (or want) me until the following week. I went to work and they told me to leave.

Compensation:

None, but I figure they still owe me for the bus fare to get there and back. Twice. (About five bucks.)

Commute:

Two buses with one transfer into a no-man's-land of broken houses on the riverfront.

Commute Time:

1 1/2 hours, each way, for a 20-minute trip

Physical Environment:

In the basement of an old church that was converted into a theatre. All in all, a very hip space. Disorganized, slightly creepy, but man! They had such a great regional reputation!

Emotional Environment:

The theatre troupe ignored me for the afternoon that I was there. I sat at a drafting table and sketched.

Nemeses:

The phantom who went through those preliminary sketches without my permission and deemed them unworthy.

Allies:

The puppets, themselves. They began to tell me what to make for them. All in one afternoon. Glorious!

Living Situation(s):

Alone. I'd moved into my own apartment right on Lark Street. It was clean, private, and had a front window that looked out over guitarists heading to their gigs and a local club owner (who wore nothing except black shorts, every day, twelve months a year) who always waved as he walked up the hill to work. The older man downstairs who collected my rent had a medical issue that involved an odorous, scabrous, tree-like growth straining from the side of his head, but he was a gentle soul and the smell improved after the surgery. My neighbor directly across the hall was a (very) angry lesbian who avoided all interaction with me whatsoever.

When I Knew:

The Puppet Fuckers may have called and asked me not to bother coming back, but I had left a brand new sketchbook behind and, besides, I was pretty angry. I stayed up all night making a hat for the sandman puppet out of dusty, brushed-lavender velvet that had a folded brim and a small silver spoon stuck through it.

Departure:

I rode the bus back to the creepy church basement. Two hours (and two transfers) later, I went in, grabbed my sketchbooks, and asked whoever-it-was behind the desk where the sandman puppet was because I'd brought him a gift. I placed the hat on the marionette's head, turned, and walked out.

What I Think About When I Think About This Damn Job:

I think of contracts and how I'll always have one for artwork in the future. I think of how smashingly smug I felt knowing I'd made something beautiful and, yet, how it didn't make any difference in the long run. Not the beauty, nor my sewing abilities, nor the overall vision. Knowing that the small hat I'd made was good and that, with enough sustained interest, I could probably turn out a better marionette than theirs (one, say, with considerably less puppet-mouth). How, later on, I became close to others who'd worked in that theater and was told that The Puppet Fuckers were considered incredibly weird and that no one really wanted to work for them.

Freshman Dining Hall, Super Wicked Old College

Employee:

FAXBoy

Location:

Schenectady, New York (Say it: "Skin-Neck-Titty")

Approximate Tenure:

1990 - 1994

Position Held:

Line Server

AKA:

Drunk Guy with Spatula

Elapsed Time Before Job Search Resumed:

I didn't look because I had to finish skool. (Somehow.)

Compensation:

$6.32/hour, FREE TUITION, and all the institutional slop I could stomach

Commute:

I could damn near fall out of whatever bed I was in and walk to work from wherever I was the night before.

Commute Time:

Ten minutes (tops)

Physical Environment:

I spent most of my time sweating my balls off behind a steam table (staring at students who didn't realize and/or want to acknowledge that I also took classes towards the same degree). There were miles of red ceramic tiling made muddy by years of dirty mop water, plenty of (sometimes) blazingly bright fluorescent lighting, and everything else was made of stainless steel.

Emotional Environment:

Kinda familial, actually. When you spend fifty or sixty hours a week with the same people, you get pretty tight (in a loosely-associated kind of way).

Nemeses:

A big-haired bitch named Glitch, customers (AKA, peers/colleagues/fellow students)

Allies:

Everybody else besides that bitch named Glitch

Living Situation(s):

Various locations throughout the city of Schenectady, including: A rooming house full of recently-divorced men on Union Street and a spacious apartment with two (or three, depending) ridiculously wealthy students on University Place

When I Knew:

I was going great guns for a couple of years, but the early, late, and long hours on top of skool started to wear on me, as did the customers who were, for the most part, incredibly spoiled children living "independently" for the first time in their lives.

Departure:

Very drunken during graduation week. I think that I just stopped showing up for work while I drank my weight in grain alcohol and Golden Anniversary every night.

What I Think About When I Think About This Damn Job:

Working the grill one Sunday morning whacked out on acid, a chick who nicknamed herself "Crack Baby" who sometimes showed up for brunch on roller skates (and really did seem to have some severe cognitive issues), being stared down by the largest rat I've ever seen out by the Dumpster one night. Clocking out at one of my dumb-ass managers during the dinner rush and yelling, "You can't make me go back in there! You can't make me go back in there!" from the back parking lot. An incredible baked-potato fight one night (and the satisfying "thud!" that they made when they hit the walls) and spitting viscously into a hockey player's stack of pancakes after he gave me a hassle one morning. A guy we called "Sarge" (because he had actually served in Viet Nam) who would hit the floor every time someone dropped a pot or there was some other equally-sudden-and-loud noise.

The svelte and suave chef who sounded like Sammy Davis, Jr., always wore a black Kangol, and never raised his voice (no matter what shit was hitting which fan). Getting hassled in the back of classrooms by "colleagues" who wanted me to whip up burgers and fries for them during the lecture because they thought it was funny that I had a job. How grateful I was for the walk-in cooler on hot days or while I was peeling metric tonnes of onions. Working with Laverne & Shirley in the bakery sometimes at, like, four or five in the morning still completely drunk and/or high from the night "before" (mmm, sprinkles and cakes). Doral cigarettes. Meat, heat, and my achin' feet!

Sasha of Luxembourg

Employee:

FileGrrl

Location:

Schenectady, New York

Approximate Tenure:

The summer of 1992

Position Held:

Stitcher

AKA:

That Slow New Girl

Elapsed Time Before Job Search Resumed:

One month

Compensation:

Piece work

Commute:

A sprint through The Old City

Commute Time:

15 minutes (if I ran fast enough)

Physical Environment:

They call it a "sweatshop" for a reason. We'd leave the doors open to the street for extra ventilation, but it didn't help. Much. I loved this small-ish, antique, brick building. The design and cutting teams worked upstairs while the first floor was full of machines (old and new, industrial and personal) as if the owner had brought in all of her high-end units from home to get the job done. I loved her.

Emotional Environment:

Fast and miserable. Everyone from Pakistan sewed like the Dickens. (I wished I could have kept up!) On good days, I was in The Zone. When this happened, the owner herself would cross the room, tally my piece counts, and tell me I was doing well. On bad days, I'd lose my concentration (dreaming up my own designs) and my piece-counts wouldn't be enough to feed me for the week. I fit in nowhere.

Nemeses:

Self. Where to begin?

Allies:

The owner who kept me on, in spite of the fact that she often said things like: "You are a good stitcher, but you will never make any money" and "It's up to you whether or not you stay. I don't have anyone else to fill the machine." I could only stitch 80 - 90 or so sleeves per hour to everyone else's 120 - 150.

Living Situation(s):

I spent the summer in a crumbling house with my boyfriend's father, who'd returned from his self-described "Swiss Chalet" in the mountains somewhere, to live "in the city" for the season. The house was filthy. I loved it and scrubbed it day-and-night to no avail.

When I Knew:

Well, it was pretty self-evident.

Departure:

I have no recollection of leaving, or staying, or of being let go.

What I Think About When I Think About This Damn Job:

The fast machines and how I loved them. How the designer/label-owner was as fabulous as her name sounded and that she was actually from the country listed on her label.

How, as the week progressed, the rhinestone-encrusted suits and hot-pink skirts would fill the circumference of the room, making it bright, cheerful, and cramped and how empty the room would be on Monday morning after the truck had taken everything to New York City on Friday night. I could see and feel the pride of production around the room, but I couldn't participate because I was constantly reminded that I'd failed to contribute my fair share. I couldn't figure out how to do it any faster. I liked sewing and making things with my hands, but the environment in this factory was not for me. Instead, I turned my attention to the theater.

Continuing Studies, Super Wicked Old College

Employee:

FAXBoy

Location:

Schenectady, New York (Say It!)

Approximate Tenure:

Summers and a few random semesters from 1990 – 1994 (and on into 1995 even?)

Position Held:

Student Assistant

AKA:

House Drunk

Elapsed Time Before Job Search Resumed:

I loved this job! (In fact, I wish I could get it back RIGHT NOW.)

Compensation:

$7($8?)/hour

Commute:

Three or four blocks on foot

Commute Time:

Five minutes in the fall and spring semesters. 10-to-15 during the winter term.

Physical Environment:

Sort of like working in the living room of someone's home-office in a swanky, historically-significant building.

Emotional Environment:

Like being the oldest, and wildest, child in a family who lived in the aforementioned swanky home (but only from Monday through Friday).

Nemeses:

Graduate students

Allies:

Squirrely

Living Situation(s):

I worked here for years, so I lived (chronologically) in a rooming house, in a strange summer sublet on Gillespie, and then in a really nice flat (with a washer and motherfucking dryer!) with two-to-four other guys on University Avenue.

When I Knew:

When I graduated, I knew that I wanted to go elsewhere (like, say, France). While I was working towards my degree, however, I never really looked for another position because everyone in the office (students excluded) was so fun to work with!

Departure:

Drunk, but ridiculously celebratory! In retrospect, I wonder if they were just glad to be rid of me(?) I don't think so, though. It took me a while to get out of skool (I had one-to-three jobs each semester for four years to get that piece of paper) and the women in this office really helped me to make it through to the end of all that nonsense and foolishness.

What I Think About When I Think About This Damn Job:

Snow falling on campus on the days when I worked in the office alone (mostly over-time on the weekends, I'm assuming). Extended, and leisurely, smoke breaks on the porch with Squirrely during the summer months. Tormenting the payroll admin by putting snap dragons (those tiny Chinese explosives) in her stapler, moving and then gluing her stuff to the top of her desk, and screwing with the hydraulics of her office chair.

Literally wanting to kill one of the little shits enrolled in the summer "enrichment" program every. g*ddamn. year! Thinking that I would never, ever graduate. Wondering how many gallons of beer, and how many fields of tobacco, I personally consumed while earning said degree. Thinking that a college degree in English might actually land me some gainful employment somewhere after graduation.

Famous Vaudeville Theater
(New York)

Employee:

FileGrrl

Location:

Schenectady, New York

Approximate Tenure:

One hellish week in the spring of 1993

Position Held:

Temporary Administrative Secretary

AKA:

That Stupid Girl

Elapsed Time Before Job Search Resumed:

A New York Minute

Compensation:

$7.00/hour(-ish)? I was ecstatic! (For a minute.)

Commute:

A scenic walk through the historic downtown district to the theater

Commute Time:

About 12 minutes

Physical Environment:

A recently restored Vaudeville theater. Upstairs, in an old office that had not been restored recently, full of furniture from the 50s that had seen better days. More like an ugly *film-noir* movie set than an office, actually, with a six-line phone that never stopped ringing. *And every call was an* **EMERGENCY!** By this time I'd worked in nursing homes, a hospital, and a domestic violence shelter and I can assure you that *nothing* in theater is an "emergency." (Especially when there isn't a show that night.)

Emotional Environment: Everyone treated me as if I were mentally disabled from the get-go. I'm not sure why. They had a woman with horrid BO, a beard, and a plaid-and-flannel-only wardrobe stacking files on a desk behind me. I thought, *"Wow! I'm going to work in the office of a famous theater -- I think I'll gussy it up!"* So I showered, used deodorant, and wore a matching skirted suit *and* Chanel #5 each day (as any decent secretary would). Nevertheless, something about me irritated the life out of the head mistress and her henchmen. I'm surprised I lasted the week and it's one of those jobs where I've always felt, in retrospect, that someone very different from me would have been able to turn that particular gig into a full-time job.

Nemeses:

The phone: All six lines. Who came up with that? Is having six lines and one person to answer them really all that productive for a company? How about *one* line and, if it's busy, the person on the other end can call the fuck back? I'm not going to get to them any time sooner anyway, and if I do answer, and then take another call, and yet another and another, by the time I get to the original caller, by now five calls deep, I am going to forget everything about it and everything that the first person said in the first place! Honestly. By the end of the week, I was just hanging up on people. It was a really horrible experience.

Allies:

My then-boyfriend. He'd worked for the same theater a few years prior and was able to explain the inter-office politics to me (somewhat). I had to ask him why they were all so damnably miserable and he explained that it was partly due to the money situation. He was bemused that the greasy-haired woman was still working in the office, but then said, "They'll probably never let her go." I wondered if I went in wearing stained sweat pants and refused to bathe if they'd hire me back.

Living Situation(s):

With my consoling sweetheart in a decrepit old house in a long-forgotten historic district full of flowers.

When I Knew:

When I got on the phone and politely asked someone who they were and they explained to me, through clenched teeth, that they'd just told me who they were. I promptly sent the call to the wrong office. By mid-morning of Day 1, I'd started frantically scribbling on a notepad what party was on which line, and whom they were asking for, but it never quite worked out exactly. By mid-afternoon of Day 2, I was in tears.

Departure:

There's a reason they're called "temp jobs."

What I Think About When I Think About This Damn Job:

How nice I looked and smelled. Going out for lunch and grabbing a magazine and some beauty products. Almost, maybe once, having a pleasant conversation with one of the administrative henchmen. The evil, evil directress and her ugly clothes. The phone ringing off the hook, quite literally. Being treated as if I were extremely stupid, and somehow meeting and/or exceeding those extremely low expectations. The sweet relief of Friday.

Development Office, Super Wicked Old College

Employee:

FAXBoy

Location:

Schenectady, New York (C'mon, you know you want to...)

Approximate Tenure:

Part of the 1994 or 1995 spring semester(?)

Position Held:

Student Intern

AKA:

Telephonic Panhandler

Elapsed Time Before Job Search Resumed:

I was very, very drunk and may have been very, very drunk while I was on the phone with distinguished alumni of this Super Wicked Old College, but I don't really remember. Point being, I was barely holding on to this job, so I didn't have enough extra time and/or mental capacity to look for anything better.

Compensation:

$7/hour (tops)

Commute:

Three or four blocks on foot

Commute Time:

Five minutes in the fall and spring semesters. 10-to-15 during the winter term.

Physical Environment:

There were a half-dozen of us crammed into the attic of another old home that was converted into office space. It was chock full of muted wall-to-wall carpeting, crown moulding, and overly-complicated phones. The space was really cramped and it was stifling on days that were, in reality, only slightly above freezing outside.

Emotional Environment:

I think I may have been the only guy and, thus, the only gay guy in an office full of career-obsessed young women. (Oh, and I couldn't even spell "career" at the time because I just. didn't. care.) So, I was like some sort of exotic drug-addled pet who somehow got himself hired into this estrogenfest.

Nemeses:

Alumni

Allies:

The "Fuck Off" button on the phone that allowed me to disconnect from the worst of my calls.

Living Situation(s):

I think I was living in an apartment with The Ex-Boyfriend and two or three other students, but I may have been living in a house full of freaks in the historic district. (I had a clusterfuck of jobs at this skool, so some of the details have blurred and grayed over time like an old Polaroid trapped under a snow bank that emerges, worse-for-wear, during a January thaw.)

When I Knew:

Like I said, I didn't know much at the time, but I knew that I didn't like talking to strangers on the phone while they were having dinner five nights a week.

Departure:

It's possible that I made it through the entire semester of this terrible internship and just drank my last paycheck on my last day somewhere (probably wondering where my next paycheck was going to come from, but not giving a rat's ass on some level, either).

What I Think About When I Think About This Damn Job:

Serial conversations that went like this:

Me: "Hello, my name is — "

Distinguished Alum #1: "No."

Me: "Hi, I'm calling from — "

Distinguished Alum #2: "No."

Me: "Good evening, would you.?."

Distinguished Alum #3: "No."

Me: "I think we were disconnected before — "

Distinguished Alum #1's wife: "Fuck off!"

Me: "I think we were disconnected before—"

Distinguished Alum #2's wife: "STOP calling here."

Me: "I think we were disconnected before—"

Distinguished Alum #3's wife: "So help me g*d, we will never give a DIME to that damn school."

And after an entire shift of this bullshit, I'd have to sit with the manager of this mini-call center who would ask me why I hadn't "made my numbers" for the day. I wanted to say, "You try talking to these bitches for more than four seconds!" It was like trying to ride one mechanical bull after another.

Last Gasp Furniture & Interiors

Employee:

FAXBoy

Location:

Schenectady, New York (OK, fuck it. Never mind…)

Approximate Tenure:

A few days in the summer of 1992, 1993, 1994, or 1995 (Pick one. Whatever works for you, works for me, too.)

Position Held:

Stock Clerk

AKA:

Sitting Duck in a Shooting Gallery at a Summer Carnival

Elapsed Time Before Job Search Resumed:

As is the case with many of the jobs that I've held in my life, I was so incredibly drunk while I worked here that I was barely aware that I was actually employed, so I was incapable of simultaneously looking for another job.

Compensation:

$5/hour (On second thought, I don't know that I even made that much...)

Commute:

Around the corner

Commute Time:

59 seconds

Physical Environment:

Last Gasp Furniture & Interiors was really a type of a performance space where the production always starred me and the cadaverous old woman who ran the place (she was always impeccably dressed for business in the 1940s and I was usually wearing my clothes from the night before). The building was a squat box of solid brick with huge windows on its front façade through which the throngs of potential customers who walked by each day could catch a bit of the show. But I'm totally lying about the throngs. There were no people then and there are even less now.

Emotional Environment:

Like being an actor, who has never read Sartre, in a lost play by Sartre.

Nemeses:

The old woman who sounded like The Ghost of Christmas Past, large dining-room tables

Allies:

Jack Daniels, Captain Morgan, Sam Adams, Jim Beam, Bartles & Jaymes

Living Situation(s):

Around the corner in a rooming house full of recently-divorced men who now fought, like clockwork, with their new girlfriends every Friday and Saturday night.

When I Knew:

Within minutes of starting on my first day…

Departure:

Quick, but totally unexpected by the old woman who called me for days after I failed to materialize to "find out when I might be back in to the shop(pe)?" Sometimes I was tempted to pick up the phone while she was leaving her messages just to whisper, "Nevermore…"

What I Think About When I Think About This Damn Job:

The extreme datedness of the crushed-velvet décor when I started. The weight and heft of the furniture that I had to move during my handful of shifts as her sole employee. The absurd and unpredictable whims of the old woman who thought that by keeping her inventory in a constant state of motion, that she might sell some of it and stay in business longer than she did.

The staircases on the back wall that led to symmetrical landings where the *artiste* worked her magic creating dining and kitchen *tableaux* for hypothetical families (while I sweat my balls off). Wondering why some of the painters who tried to sell their work at this place ever picked up a paintbrush in the first place (and if they might have all been blind to begin with)? I'll never know the answer to these questions as the shop(pe) now sits dangerously vacant with a sign posted to the front door warning potential trespassers about the asbestos within and the instability of the structure. That her hair was fireproof even then.

1-(800)-GET-MEDZ

Employee:

FileGrrl

Location:

Glenville, New York

Approximate Tenure:

Three months in the fall of 1994

Position Held:

Phone Scab

AKA:

Phone Scab

Elapsed Time Before Job Search Resumed:

I relaxed for a bit on this one, as it was the early 90s and having a three-month gig close to where I lived was like being rich. I bought food for the first time in several months. I mean, WOW! I was employed!

Compensation:

A whopping $5.90/hour! (Unheard of in those days.)

Commute:

A short drive over the bridge to a town I'd never heard of.

Commute Time:

10 Minutes

Physical Environment:

Cube. Not quite a Cube City, more like a Cube Village.

Emotional Environment:

Cubed. I wasn't well-versed in phone customer service at this time. I got over it quickly. I was very nervous, as the phones were referred to as "live" (as if they were power lines that were going to electrocute me). I was terrified of speaking to strangers without knowing what their demands were going to be, so working in a call center wasn't exactly the ideal job for me. We were hired to replace people as the company had relocated its call center to Virginia, hence, the people who'd been on phone duty for years (and all knew each other from high school and had been there long enough to have decorated their cubes in kitsch) all left one-by-one, to find other work (Or not.)

I thought finding another job was a smart idea, but since I never really found employment without help, I stayed put. There was a nice lunchroom and, except for the phone, it looked like it had been a nice place to work. Mostly, though, I just felt like a scab from *Norma Rae*; only instead of the union coming in to fight for the rights of the workers, the workers were dropping like flies. There was no way to make friends. We were separated across enemy lines: Those Who Were Rightfully Employed vs. Those Who Were Brought in to Replace Them as the former filed out during a rather long, dreary Christmas season. ((Sigh.))

Nemeses:

The phone

Allies:

FAXBoy. We met during training while the company was teaching us the elaborate phone system, monitoring our every word, and forcing us to up-sell vitamins to customers who just needed a prescription refilled.

He had a blond flattop, looked like he'd just graduated from The Super Wicked Old College nearby, and had landed his first temp gig on the way to a very lucrative career as a stockbroker (just as soon as Dad found a place for him at the firm). Successful, beer-drinking, football-watching. I hated him and wrote him off immediately.

Living Situation:

I was living with a man I loved who'd suddenly stopped having sex with me. The house we were in was comfortable, if messy. My cats were happy, but I was distraught.

When I Knew:

I knew two things at this job: 1) That it was temporary from the get-go, and 2) That I didn't want to lose FAXBoy. Yet, lose him I did, as one day he left our cube ranch without so much as a paper airplane launched my way to tell me where he'd be.

Departure:

Merry Christmas Eve! Go home, cattle, and don't ever come back! Your work is FINISHED.

What I Think About When I Think About This Damn Job:

The little butterfly collage I made from old magazines in my cube. Dressing as a belly dancer for Halloween. Meeting FAXBoy. Sending paper airplanes over the tops of our cubes that contained info about local arts events and what we were reading/listening to after they separated us for being disruptive. Him begging his then-partner, "Please don't leave me here." FAXBoy's sudden disappearance that left me alone for that last, long month. Damn him.

1-(800)-GET-MEDZ

Employee:

FAXBoy

Location:

Schenectady, New York

Approximate Tenure:

Two months in the fall of 1994

Position Held:

Seasonal Customer Service Representative

AKA:

Temp Slave/Telephonic Cannon Fodder

Elapsed Time Before Job Search Resumed:

Unfortunately, I was too drunk to look for another job while I had this one.

Compensation:

$6/hour(?)

Commute:

I got a ride to work every day with The Ex-Boyfriend.

Commute Time:

Three-to-five minutes, but I was often late because of my highly unreliable driver.

Physical Environment:

A massive warehouse without windows somewhere off of Erie Boulevard full of stale carbon dioxide, nicotine, and tar from all the smokers talking on all of the phones. Bigger than a football field and darker than black lung.

Emotional Environment:

Like a coal mine.

Nemeses:

The really fucking cranky old people on the other end of the phone.

Allies:

FileGrrl!

Living Situation(s):

In a big flat on University Place with The Ex-Boyfriend, two roommates from The Super Wicked Old College, and a psychotic little Vietnamese pot-bellied pig.

When I Knew:

I knew immediately that I wasn't long for this assignment, but I didn't have the mad skillz at the time to get out as fast as I would have really liked. (Like, say, shortly after day one).

Departure:

Abrupt and without warning. I just couldn't bear to go in one day, so I didn't, but I also didn't bother to tell anyone, either, choosing instead to simply disappear like a rusty ship in The Bermuda Triangle of Tempness.

What I Think About When I Think About This Damn Job: Begging The Ex-Boyfriend not to drop me off every single day of this (partial) assignment ("If you really loved me, you would have taken me back home!" was one of my favorite parting shots before I slammed the car door.) Reading *The Wasteland* while taking phone orders, but putting callers on hold for minutes at a time to better wade through Elliot's thick verse. Having one customer ask me "where that nice young woman went [and] why [was I] so stupid?" and responding that, "Well, ma'am, they were looking for stupid young men, so I applied for the job, and now I'm stuck talking to you" (I think I was training another temp at the time, as well, and he/she/it (meaning the temp) nearly fell out of his/her/its folding chair behind me). Laying eyes on FileGrrl from across the lunchroom one day and recognizing her inherent evilness before we even exchanged our first words. Talking to a man who was having trouble with his hearing after jamming suppositories in his ears and speaking with a very entertaining woman who wanted some extra-large rubbers to slap on her extra horny old man. Standing on my desk with an intricately-folded paper airplane cocked in my right hand (I mean, really, this sucker verged on motherfuckin' Origami) as a gaggle of management walked by days before my departure. Returning to the temp agency (with FileGrrl for moral support) to pick up my last paycheck and having the receptionist admonish me for not calling and/or not writing and responding, "Nope, now give me my money." Having to ask every raisin if they "wanted vitamins with that?" every time one of them placed a rheumy order.

The Next Generation

Employee:

FAXBoy

Location:

Schenectady, New York

Approximate Tenure:

One night only in the fall of 1994

Position Held:

Stripper

AKA:

Half-Naked Mess

Elapsed Time Before Job Search Resumed:

When I took the stage, I wasn't exactly taking a bold step forward into a glorious new future, so I was hardly thinking about what I might do next, above-and-beyond taking my clothes off in front of a bunch of drunk locals for money.

Compensation:

$33 in tips w/unlimited weed and tequila. No medical, no dental.

Commute:

A half-a-block on foot

Commute Time:

Literally a minute

Physical Environment:

loud, Loud, LOUD! And all sorts of wrong. It was a grungy strip club in a half-dead town and the building (an old brick fire house), as well as the full-time employees, looked that much worse for the wear.

Emotional Environment:

I was drunk as a fuck and higher than a mother, so I may have checked my emotions at the door.

Nemeses:

José Cuervo, THC, Curiosity

Allies:

(Most) everyone in the audience, the actual strippers in the basement who prepped me for my illustrious début

Living Situation(s):

In The Big House of Freaks with FileGrrl, The Ex-Boyfriend, and The Mathematician (and all of their cats)

When I Knew:

Oh, I always knew that I wouldn't get a call back to this particular temp job…

Departure:

Abrupt and raucous after we left the stage and put our clothes back on.

What I Think About When I Think About This Damn Job:

That, in retrospect, it was quite easy to see how masterfully we got played. Here's how it went down: The Mathematician and I were drinking heavily at The Gay Bar (which was equidistant from The Biker Bar and The Next Generation) in order to overcome some of the boredom of our studies and in attempt to forget the fact that we lived in the crap-ass town that we did. After a few hours of soaking our brains in the fun juice, the older, slightly hagilicious woman sitting next to us asked us if we wanted to make some money. (Of course we did!) When she explained the terms and conditions of her offer to us (a little Jack-&-Jill action at the strip club down the street), The Mathematician told her that we were both horribly disfigured from the neck down. But we were suckered in by a few free shots, a bit of flattery, and by the thrill of something new and (potentially) exciting.

The Next Generation

Employee:

FileGrrl

Location:

Schenectady, New York

Approximate Tenure:

One mad evening in the winter of 1995

Position Held:

Dancer

AKA:

Dancer

Elapsed Time Before Job Search Resumed:

One minute

Compensation:

$2.00 in tips

Commute:

A short walk to the wrong side of the tracks

Commute Time:

10 minutes

Physical Environment:

Somewhat dirty

Emotional Environment:

I was the early entertainment for the evening, as the system to hire new dancers was to make an appearance on Amateur Night, dance one's clothes off and see what the dance manager said afterward. Pretty standard. I figured if it worked out, I could make some easy money. Dancing is easy and the music was good (as I got to select my own choice Rolling Stones, Nine Inch Nails, and Sisters of Mercy faves). The emotional fall-out from becoming a dancer is actually quite complicated, however. There is an immediate rush of gratification: *I'm a stripper! Woooo-Hoo!* Which instantly morphs into a seedy form of "hot." It doesn't have to be seedy, though. I've since learned that just about anywhere else in the world, there are bars upon bars where beautiful girls take it all off for loads of cash, pay their way through school, and call it done. However, in Upstate New York, all forms of sex are still considered "dirty" (somehow) due to some bizarre clusterfuck of English/Dutch/Victorian/ghetto repression that still lingers north of Manhattan. There was my fantasy of what I really wanted (and needed) stripping to be and then there was the reality. Reality being one lone guy sitting front-and-center who paid one lone dollar to sniff my one lone pussy (which I found appalling) and another dollar from the friend who accompanied me and gave me a tip because he felt sorry that I'd taken (most of) it off for a buck. Any actual "sniffing" was not something I'd been prepared for. I'd watched the dancer before me, a regular, and figured out quickly that just such a nasal favor was standard operating procedure. Until that point, I figured that you just danced and that was that.

Nemeses:

The customer. His nose.

Allies:

FAXBoy's man at the time, sitting at the bar and clapping at appropriate moments. The music. The dance manager. The other dancers (who were old hands at it by the time I washed up on this particular shore). They had a small, crummy, poorly-lit dressing room sequestered backstage that was knee-deep in every manner of thong, bra, pasty, makeup, stiletto, feather boa, flimsy skirt, and hair spray that a girl could want. It was like stepping into your best friend's bedroom (if your best friend happened to be a narcissistic, bi-polar, drag-queen stripper). Part of it was very enjoyable: they shared their clothes, makeup tips, drug-store perfume, and Band-Aids for their nipples. They were very open in their attitudes about sex and about dancing, yet part of it was slightly gross: *You share what? Who washes these things?* And, ultimately, that these young women with their open attitudes and their great bodies were relegated to the back room of a crappy club on North Jay Street instead of being elevated to a higher status to, say, that of courtesan or highly-paid mistress in Paris or New York City told me a whole lot about self esteem, as well as the social conventions and lack of openness in the hinterlands.

Living Situation(s):

With FAXBoy, his man, and The Mathematician in The House of Freaks. I lived in the library of this small (dilapidated, rented) mansion.

When I Knew:

Perhaps it was the club, but I really didn't need to bring myself or my female parts in such close proximity to anyone, let alone a perfect stranger.

After my time onstage was over, I was given a performance review by the dance manager. She told me to lose ten-to-twenty pounds ("the men are mean, it's just the way it is, but it will work off fast, honey, don't worry…"), that I had "great tits," and could I "please come in to work as a topless waitress for the Busty McCoy show on Tuesday night?" She really needed "some girls."

Departure:

I said I'd think about it, shoved my hard-earned dollar bills into my bra, tossed back a shot of Jack Daniel's (courtesy of my chaperone), and left.

What I Think About When I Think About This Damn Job:

How my life choices began to chase after me. How fantasies and reality tend to get all jumbled up and, in fact, create one's "reality." How fine I looked in a red Victoria's Secret set that night.

The Electric City Café

Employee:

FAXBoy

Location:

Schenectady, New York

Approximate Tenure:

1994 - 1995

Position Held:

Barista/Assistant Manager

AKA:

Ringmaster

Elapsed Time Before Job Search Resumed:

I didn't look until I got fired

Compensation:

$3.35/hour plus tips, food, coffee, and random drawings that regulars left for me after their "shifts" ended

Commute:

Five blocks from The House of Freaks

Commute Time:

Five minutes (max)

Physical Environment:

A wide open space full of small tables with one big round one that we called "The Captain's Table" set in front of the display of coffee beans across from the register. It was done up in pre-St*rFux coffee tones, but they weren't obnoxious and the artwork on the walls (sometimes impressive, often atrocious) was mostly made by the regulars.

Emotional Environment:

It got real homey, real quick, and sometimes it felt something like walking into your best friend's living room on some days when I showed up for work. There was a fair amount of responsibility and heavy lifting involved, but I never felt unsure about what I should, or should not, be doing.

Nemeses:

Bubbles (the corpulent transvestite who had a thing for wearing gold plastic mules) and the army of rehabbers who demanded five-star service, but never tipped. (Ever.)

Allies:

Everyone, except the rehabbers

Living Situation(s):

In a rented three-story house in the historic district full of freaks that included FileGrrl, The Mathematician, and The Ex-Boyfriend.

When I Knew:

When I walked in one day and got the cold shoulder from EVERYONE. I was like, "Who the fuck died in here?" and, when nobody answered, I knew it was *real* bad.

Departure:

Completely unexpected and unbelievably nasty. After the icy reception, I got called into the office in the basement and was asked very pointedly if I: "Knew what 'liability' meant"? I was like, "What the fuck, Don?"

Apparently, someone in the audience of the previous night's open mic poetry reading took offense at the fact that one of the freakier poets had thrown a chair, a pack of cigarettes, and a fork (maybe a spoon(?)) into the enraptured crowd during his performance and complained to management before my shift started the next day. (No one lost an eye, or was hit in the head by any flying furniture, so I didn't think twice about the reading, because this guy was one of dozens of poets and performance artists who read and performed the night before under my (alleged) watch.) I was livid. I swore. (A lot.) I took my final paycheck to The Gay Bar up the street and drank it all away within hours.

What I Think About When I Think About This Damn Job: Thinking that this was the way to longevity at a job by getting in on the ground floor. I had helped clean out the raw space, then painted the walls of the café with my friends from The Super Wicked Old College who opened it, and then moved in the very furniture that would ultimately get me fired. Knowing that I was a fuck-up while I was getting fired. I often drank my way through night shifts by hiding bottles of wine (or 40 ounces) in the rows of flavored syrups meant for specialty coffee beverages and Italian sodas. After the bosspeople (now divorced) left for the day, I'd just pluck my poison from the ranks of Torani® bottles and jump into the disarray that a night shift always brought with it. There wasn't much else going on in this one-café town, so everyone ended up at this place after dark and it was like a big party until I kicked everyone out (usually by playing Hole's "Rock Star" at them at great volume).

Showing all of my friends' artwork and some of them doing coke in the basement during their openings. The daily DRAAAH-MAAAAAH involving both patrons and employees (and sometimes patrons and employees at the same time). The fascinating physicist who sat in the far corner in a worn pinstripe suit by himself every day crunching numbers for some unknown university publisher while cultivating a fantastic ZZ-Topesque beard. Prince and his revolution. The nametag left as a tip by The Pink-Haired Dyke that read, "I Hate You All," that I wore proudly from that day forward. Laughing noncommittally, and somewhat maniacally, when newbies or out-of-towners asked me if that was "really true?" when they read it. The fact that The Ex-Boyfriend and The Mathematician were also hired-and-fired at The Electric City Café. Listening to FileGrrl read her poetry on another open mic night and being so proud, so happy.

Insurance Agency

Employee:

FileGrrl

Location:

Schenectady, New York

Approximate Tenure:

One month during the O.J. Simpson trial, October, 1995

Position Held:

FileGrrl

AKA:

FileGrrl. Is, was, and shall always be: FileGrrl (as there was absolutely no movement up in this company).

Elapsed Time Before Job Search Resumed:

Well, technically, I didn't look. I just left, letting the chips fall where they may.

Compensation:

Was I paid?

Commute:

A quick zip in my own car (amazing!) from my apartment to a dumb office park, where I frequently turned into the wrong parking area because they all looked the same (unless I counted the driveways or used the large sculpture on the side lawn to navigate my way through the visual monotony).

Commute Time:

About twenty minutes, give or take 600 traffic lights and 8,429 other drivers all going to the same office park.

Physical Environment:

A wide-open pool of desks with no cubes or bookshelves to protect us. There were just six desks, all face-to-face, with three to a side (luckily, I got to sit across from a really nice lady). If we'd been skeet lining up to be shot we would have made really easy targets.

It was my first experience with an open office set-up and I vowed never again. (This type of environment seems to be just fine for many people, although I could make a strong argument against it being the right environment for anyone. It has certainly never worked out for me.) The work, itself, was to sort piles and piles and piles of paper insurance claims into plastic alpha sorters. The sorters, themselves, were at a premium. Some were good, but a couple of them were broken, missing the all-important "Mc" combo, or an "E," or both, making the sorting worse than it already was. Early birds got complete alpha sorters, but late girls (who flew with the bats at night) would be missing "Mc" and/or "E" all day long. The nice lady and I had it worked out that whoever got there first would grab two decent sorters and give one to the other when she arrived. After we sorted all morning, we went to the rows upon rows of filing cabinets. A person could be lost in there for hours. I had no patience for the sorting, the filing, or the hierarchy of high school bitches who ruled the office. I'd gone to college to get a degree, but I ended up moving to a city where the population that had skipped school was now in charge of all of the crappy jobs that were available to me. This team drank beer, tanned, and discussed sports. Their HR "department" was made up of a single blond bombshell who wore very short pink and blue matching suits with high heels and acted as though she felt sorry for me when she was forced to deal with me. Obviously, no good behavior on my part was ever going to move me up in this company.

Emotional Environment:

Total fishbowl living. I was dirt. There were five other temps besides me, but I felt like The Lowest of the Low because I'd already stopped aspiring. I saw how it really was.

Nemeses:

The Class of 1988 who easily snapped up the better positions and then got to tell me what to do. (The pecking order was amazing!) If I'd purchased a red, white, and blue pick-up truck out of high school and become instantaneously pregnant, I'd have been much better off and been rewarded for my good behavior with a fairly easy desk job in an office full of cronies who also raised babies, drank beer constantly, and watched ballgames on TV on weekends.

Allies:

The really nice lady stationed across from me, whose young son had been diagnosed with cancer the previous year, who came in one day and told me that she wasn't staying, that it was a crappy job, and that she was leaving. After her son finally got better, she realized that life was precious and short and not meant to be spent in an office filing papers for stupid bar hags. She was gone the next day.

Living Situation(s):

In a row house apartment with a man who had no interest in me and our adventurous roommate, Walter.

Walter, having arrived from farmland in the New York outback, was quite green, but we showed him all of the best movies, rotten books, and radical ideas that we could.

When I Knew:

Soon after the nice lady's departure, I ended up in the stacks with my morning's sorting slipping and sliding all over the place, and my skirt, stockings, and skin catching on the corners of the filing cabinet drawers. I stopped, tossed a pile of claims on the floor, and was surprised by how good it felt. Then I threw a few into the air and that felt even better. I told administrative passersby that this was a stupid job. "Meaningless." "Mindless." "Numbing!"

Departure:

After this declaration of independence, I was the one gone the next day. I neglected to inform them that they just weren't working out for me.

What I Think About When I Think About This Damn Job:

That life *is* way too short to work on the same boring task, over and over again, until Friday finally comes. The way old copy paper moves through stale air and trapped sunlight.

Regional HMO

Employee:

FAXBoy

Location:

Latham, New York

Approximate Tenure:

1995 – 1996

Position Held:

Marketing Clerk

AKA:

FAXBoy

Elapsed Time Before Job Search Resumed:

Believe it or not, I actually kinda liked this one.

Compensation:

$8.9765239838239351239844128939 65/hour, healthcare(!), and unlimited long distance calls and FAX transmissions on company time

Commute:

On some Troy-Schenectady bus up from the hood, but most days I crawled down the steps of my crumbling brownstone into the heated (or air-conditioned) style of a friend's old Olde_Mobile (the middle 's' had fallen off of the trunk long before).

Commute Time:

On the bus: Anywhere from 45 minutes to three hours. In the car: 13 minutes (tops) door-to-door (even in a knock down, drag out, Northeast blizzard) as my friend was a Formula 1 racer.

Physical Environment:

Somebody else's old office park/strip mall. Like the previous tenants had all fired themselves just before the first of the month and this particular health maintenance organization was offered a deal that they just couldn't refuse to take over the lease. They wanted to instill confidence and retrofit style onto the concrete-and-fluorescent office buildings from the 70s with crappy corporate signage from the early 90s. There was a strange bar across the parking lot ("Chaucer's"/"Shakespeare's"/Something with a vague high-school literary allusion and equally as dumb) that I never went to with my overly perky co-comrades.

Emotional Environment:

It was sort of like working in the enormous waiting room of a Soviet doctor's office, where all of the employees were patients with various ailments/diagnoses/facial tics even though there were no doctors in my building.

Nemeses:

Southern Comfort, that one severe marketing director who always administrated me while I was mid-conversation with Squishy in New York City.

Allies:

Just about everyone else in the office.

Living Situation(s):

Around the corner from The Palace Theatre in Litigation City, New York, with The Ex-Boyfriend upstairs from Lick + Riz.

When I Knew:

As mentioned, I was not immediately plotting my escape from this health factory like I usually did within the first week of any new job. People were (dare I say?) relatively nice.

Departure:

By the book (two weeks, at least!) and *very* festive --
!Olé!

What I Think About When I Think of This Damn Job:
Electronically expediting useless documents that were originally printed on sheets of dead trees and receiving inappropriate artwork from FileGrrl on said FAX machine. Accidentally dialing 911 (more than once) on the aforementioned FAX machine. Sleeping in The Library (what they often referred to as "the men's room") and being fetched by the awesome receptionists when I received personal phone calls while often passed out on a toilet in one of the stalls. The Halloween party with the enormous fake Christmas tree where my friend, Marjorie, came in a FAXBoy costume. Returning the Christmas tree to Sears after the party with one of The Freaks. When the woman behind the counter asked us why we were returning the

Halloween tree, we explained that "we forgot that we were Jewish." My "office," which was a small desk with an old phone at the end of a narrow corridor (behind a row of cubicles) where everyone picked up the mail that I sorted for them twice a day. (You took a sharp right after the FAX and copy machines and you were there!) Egg McMuffinz, "*sin carne con tomate*," that I had almost every day for breakfast in an attempt to soak up all of the alcohol that was still in my system from the night before (although it often felt like I went straight from the bar to my desk before immediately bouncing back out to get breakfast at McFuck's). The *piñata* full of cigarettes and rubbers that the office gave me as a "please go away" present for my trip across the country.

Disney's *Flopper*

Employee:

FAXBoy

Location:

Treasure Island (just off the coast of San Francisco on the way to Oakland, *arrgghh!*)

Employee:

FAXBoy

Approximate Tenure:

Five glorious days in the late summer/early fall of 1996

Position Held:

Movie Extra

AKA:

"Human Wallpaper" (I think the director actually used this term *officially* when constructing scenes!)

Elapsed Time Before Job Search Resumed:

Why would anyone want a job *other* than this one(?)

Compensation:

$12-15/hour, plus lunch and/or dinner every day

Commute:

I don't really remember how I got to that first day of shooting, but I found other rolls of human wallpaper to give me a ride back-and-forth over The Bay Bridge for the next four.

Commute Time:

Ten minutes

Physical Environment:

This was way weird: Disney constructed a FAKE basketball court on Treasure Island, despite the fact that there were perfectly good (and authentic) basketball courts in both San Francisco and Oakland that they could have used.

Emotional Environment:

Like being a Hollywood star without all of the hassles of fame or fortune

Nemeses:

Robin Williams

Allies:

Marcia Gay Harden and The Starlets from Haight Street (two blond extras who had achieved minor celebrity in a boat scene on *Nasty Britches*, a cop show (starring Don Johnson and Cheech (from *Cheech & Chong*) that had just started shooting in San Francisco)

Living Situation(s):

In a very crooked railroad apartment next to The Central Freeway on Market Street. ("Next to" is a bit misleading; this crooked railroad apartment was practically ON The Central Freeway! You could watch miscreants get pulled over by the cops for speeding right outside of the massive kitchen windows while eating your Querrio's in the morning or wave to tour buses full of Midwesterners stuck in rush-hour traffic.)

When I Knew:

Are you kidding me?!? I wanted this job to last FOR-FUCKING-EVER(!)

Departure:

Sad, perfunctory, but totally predicted by the completion of the scene we were shooting. (The cattle were simply released back into the wild after they were no longer useful.)

What I Think About When I Think About This Damn Job:

Robin Williams and his never-ending monologue. Initially, he was the big draw for this particular temp job, but then he never shut up. EVER. (Monkey Boy doesn't have an "OFF" button just in case you had your own suspicions about that particular genius...) Marcia Gay Harden, on the other hand, was a class act and very fun to hang out with. (She even sent me a glossy 8X10 after the movie came out.) Sitting for days on end in this fake arena watching fools run around with signs that told us where to look and when to look there while we watched some dumb-ass fake basketball game for three or four days (as the movie itself was a computer-generated mess). Getting upgraded to the Screen Actors Guild tent for two or three days after I told the casting company that I couldn't possibly miss my "important graduate seminars" to shoot their silly little Hollywood film (knowing full well that they needed me for continuity). Drinking all night long with The Starlets at The Gold Cane after we were let go. The tambourine that one of them left on the living room floor.

Famous Vaudeville Theatre
(San Francisco)

Employee:

FAXBoy

Location:

San Francisco, California

Approximate Tenure:

Two months in 1997

Position Held:

Perhaps "Untitled"

AKA:

Gopher/Blond Intern

Elapsed Time Before Job Search Resumed:

I was riding high on the "free" money from grad skool, so I don't think I was that concerned. HOWEVER, Ted has told me stories since then about students who have invested this "free" money while they were actually in skool and graduated into massive piles of ca$h(!) My life in hell...

Compensation:

$8/hour

Commute:

Super easy. This theatre is right across the street from Theatre DayGlo, so I just walked to work. Straight down Valencia and into the gauntlet of dealers and junkies at 16th and Mission

Commute Time:

15-to-20 minutes (depending on the severity of the hangover)

Physical Environment:

De-CAYING and OPULENT! Built in 1908 and all about the red velvet. Like The Famous Vaudeville Theater in Schenectady without the corporate facelift.

Emotional Environment:

Indoors: Really, really fun! Outdoors: An existential *Killing-an-Arab* kinda hell.

Nemeses:

Theatre-goers/patrons

Allies:

The two HIV+ beefcakes from Florida who brought this horrendous production to SF. One was the playwright and the other was the producer/director. *Muy* convenient! I guess the writer guy had had a bunch of productions in The South and thought that the time was right to take over The Left Coast. The producer may have just had some money and was funding these light, light, light musicals because he loved the writer guy.

Living Situation(s):

Market Street with The Menagerie. I think we had a pretty full house right about this time.

When I Knew:

After the second or third marketing adventure out on The Avenues with my co-worker, Steven. Steven was so nice and so sweet and my life was so fast and so furious at that point that he was an integral part of my decision to stop answering the phone when this job turned slightly sour for me.

Steven was kinda round and quiet and he had this monster of a boyfriend (named Stephen) who wracked up thousands of dollars in credit-card debt by way of Internet porn (which Steven then attempted to pay for him because he was just like that). Unfortunately, I had to hear about the ins-and-outs of this crap relationship as we ran around Geary Boulevard (and environs) trying to get all of the Russian and Chinese business owners to proudly display posters for an *über*-gay musical with an atrocious title (*Jane Loves Dick*).

Departure:

As with other departures during this era, it was a bit passive and fueled by alcohol in a way. Like, I would stay up drinking all night (and possibly bitching about my job) and wouldn't rise from the dead until well after noon so as to miss the ringing of the phone when one of my bosses called to check "my availability."

What I Think About When I Think About This Damn Job:

I think about the times that they (my beefy bosses) invited me over to their apartment for brunch before we worked all day and all night together. It was always eggs and hash browns, coffee, and orange juice and they were so NICE and I always got a bit quiet when they downed their dozens of pills without missing a beat in their own conversations. I vividly remember my first night of work when I walked into the GORGEOUS Victoria Theatre in response to an ad in *The Guardian* or *The Weekly* and spoke up to a man on a ladder who asked me to hold it for him and hired me on the spot. That night at the opening, I was a bartender and opened bottles of champagne for drunken attendees and actually hit the ceiling (at least fifty feet up) with one of the corks that went whizzing by my eye... I thought to myself, "It's all fun and games until..." Marching in The Gay Pride Parade with the awful float full of nasty actors from this production my first year in SF. I felt as if I had "arrived" in some way...

The Tucked Away Café

Employee:

FAXBoy

Location:

San Fiasco, California

Approximate Tenure:

Six weeks during the summer of 1997

Position Held:

Employee #4

AKA:

Counter Schmuck #1

Elapsed Time Before Job Search Resumed:

Six weeks

Compensation:

$0.20/week, plus tips

Commute:

A brisk walk up Octavia from Market Street into Hayes Valley. Depending on my level of inebriation or the severity of my hangover, however, this could feel like scaling Kilimanjaro.

Commute Time:

Anywhere between three and thirty minutes depending on my level of distractibility

Physical Environment:

Ridiculously kitschy interior on the first-floor of an old Victorian frosted in light pastel paints.

The décor was standard-issue San Francisco café fare (old albums, sun-faded posters of Paris and Rome, spider plants, fake flowers, and crusty postcards sent by old customers from exotic locales years before were haphazardly attached to the walls and ceiling to signify that "this place is *really* quirky and other people who have come here before you have really, really liked it").

Emotional Environment:

Homey, fo' sho', but infinitely less quirky as an employee. Sort of like being trapped in the kitchen during a family brunch at Easter. (Except that Easter is every day and lasts for six weeks.)

Nemeses:

The "Mom" side of the Mom-and-Pop equation

Allies:

The "Pop" side of the Mom-and-Pop equation

Living Situation(s):

The Market Street Commune in San Francisco with a revolving cast of residents ranging in number from three-to-thirteen at any given time for the 4+ bedroom flat perched high atop the It's Crap Diner and Grooves Records.

When I Knew:

Honestly, I wasn't broadsided by a desire to run screaming from the joint until the bitter end.

Departure:

Drunken, yet silent, meaning that I got really, really drunk for days and just never went back after "The Incident" (see next section).

What I Think About When I Think About This Damn Job:

I got this job after I hung some paintings on the wall for the first of many "solo exhibitions" in cafés, clubs, and bars all over The Bay Area. I literally hung my work, realized that I was flat broke, and then asked "The Mom" if they were hiring. A large, crusty woman who appeared to have been born into the apron she always wore hired me, but I sort of knew that I would always be on probation under her ever-watchful eye. (Her husband, however, didn't seem to really know the difference, or care to know the difference, between the handful of employees who handled the ca$h in his café.) On a good day, the front door would be open to a breeze carrying hints of eucalyptus and the foot traffic would be light enough that I could sort of relax and enjoy the free food and occasional interesting customer while I read a book. On a bad day (usually on the weekends), I would slip on a used rubber in the rain on my way up the hill and the place would be slammed as soon as I opened the door. Like, I could be the only one making hundreds of Fake McMuffinz (that were ridiculously popular at this place), lattés and cappuccinos (*cappuccini?*), running the register, keeping the regular coffee flowing, and prepping sandwiches for the lunch crowd when one of the owners would come in to survey the damage and to start their own shift.

Invariably, it was the wife and she was never thrilled by the aftermath of the morning rush and, I'm sure, by my attitude after these rushes first thing in the day. Over the course of my six-week tenure, I became annoyed with some of the customers, particularly if they attempted to place an order while they were still having a conversation on their cell phone. When this happened, I would pointedly pass them over for the next person in line and, if the person on the phone bitched or complained, I would simply explain that they "were obviously *very* busy and I didn't want to interrupt."

But then I met my match in the form of The Scrape-My-Bagel Bitch.

She arrived in a flourish of self-importance from the salon across the street almost every day and she was usually only mildly annoying, but one day she came in a bit later than usual and ordered a plain bagel, buttered, and lightly toasted. When I explained to her that we were out of plain bagels and that the only ones we had left were a batch of "everything" bagels, she told me to "scrape it and make it." [Note: "Everything" bagels are covered in poppy seeds, bits of roasted garlic, kittie litter, sprinkles of indeterminate flavors, and bits of gravel from all over North America.] I pretended like I hadn't heard her until she repeated the petulant phrase that pushed me over the edge:

"Scrape. *My*. BAGEL."

I have never felt like such a peasant.

Colossal Publishing Company #1

Employee:

FAXBoy

Location:

San Francisco, California

Approximate Tenure:

Three months during the spring term of 1998

Position Held:

Editorial Intern

AKA:

The Student That They Had To/Felt Obligated To Hire in Order to Fulfill Some Sort of Outreach/Educational Mentor/Community Service Obligation

Elapsed Time Before Job Search Resumed:

A month(?) I'm not sure that I had enough brain cells at this point to actually know what was good for me:-)

Compensation:

20 hours/week at $10/hour

Commute:

The 32 Embarcadero bus (since replaced by the beautiful, and historic, F-Line!)

Commute Time:

40+ minutes each way. You could wait forfuckingever for that #32.

Physical Environment:

Not-too-shabby, actually. Nondescript office tower tucked into the corporate foliage just off of the Embarcadero near Houston's Restaurant (famous for its meat concoctions, but also serving a strange veggie burger assemblage that was colored with organic beet juice to replicate the experience of eating something actually dead). I think they took me there on my first day(?)* Definitely during my first week, though.

Emotional Environment:

Something like being the actual child on National Take Your Child to Work Day. They made me feel welcome initially, but then had nothing for me to do, except to sit in someone's abandoned cubicle to play with the stapler and drool.

Nemeses:

The Clock and the full-time employees. They brought smug condescension to new lows.

Allies:

None

Living Situation(s):

Market Street with The Ex-Boyfriend and The Marijuana Monster

When I Knew:

When I realized that they were fucking me under the table by classifying me as an "independent contractor and/or freelancer." What this actually meant was: I would file an invoice in San Francisco, have my pre-teen boss sign it before I packaged it up to send (inter-office by mule) to New Jersey, where the bitches at HQ would sit on it for weeks, and then my paycheck would show up a month later (having been mailed to my apartment even though I was actually working in their fucking SF office). Unfortunate, as this could have been a cushy gig.

Departure:

Stealth. I just packed up what few personal belongings I had at this place, along with my brand new 400lb. dictionary, and made like I was just heading out for lunch with my backpack nearly dragging on the floor as I walked out the door. ("Be back soon..." NOT!) The Ex-Boyfriend got so annoyed at all of the phone calls where my *cajones*-less "manager" called to check my "availability" in the following weeks. "Hmm," I would think while listening to the machine ramble on and on, "I think I'm all out of that at the moment..."

What I Think About When I Think About This Damn Job:

The corporate foliage that reminded me of the Pacific Northwest, the fact that I was much shyer and much more self-conscious at the time. For instance: I had to follow up on chapter reviews with professors all over the country and I dreaded the project management of it all and speaking to this one guy at Valdosta State University in Georgia. He would give me hell because he could smell the fear through the phone. (I got over all of this at Colossal Publishing Company #2 because it was such as sink-or-swim situation.) The countless hours that I spent in the storage room (simply being "lost") reading the theoretical math texts and poring over the French books. And the countless hours that I spent listening to the lame-ass relationship woes of my stupid boss, BritKnee. BritKnee was from Colorado and considering moving back because Dave/Robert/Alexander wanted a change of scenery.

She had breast buds and I know she felt really weird having to "manage" this old gay guy who was in grad skool (also something she was considering). I *hate* being a captive audience for people like that in these stupid office environments. Like when you're stuck listening to all of this stuff about whatever boy it is, sometimes you just want to cut to the chase and say something like: "He's gay/abusive and immature and/or obviously cheating on you..." just so you don't have to listen to the Lifetime *Movie of the Week* prattle anymore. (G*d, I really AM a people person...) The numbers on the clock face of the sleek chrome Fog City Diner that were replaced with the phrase "Don't Worry." That they have rabbit on the menu and that that worried me a lot...

* This is where Louise took me for my last day (her last day?) when I worked at Colossal Publishing Company #2.

Linda's Blue Bayou

Employee:

FileGrrl

Location:

Albany, New York

Approximate Tenure:

October 2000 - December 2000

Position Held:

Cocktail Waitress/Bar Back

AKA:

The Girl with The Glasses

Elapsed Time Before Job Search Resumed:

I didn't look as I was already working at a full-time job

Compensation:

[Something] an hour, paid out at the end of the night, plus tips. Some nights, I brought home more than the dancers. This was especially true on rainy nights, when the men wouldn't come out. Dancing is not nearly as lucrative as everyone thinks. It really depends on the club. In some, you can get your start on stage and then move on to a better club. Others are high-end from the get-go. It really depends on the owner's attitude towards the girls and the customers. (And the location, of course.)

Commute:

A short drive from uptown to downtown, from a version of normality to a much seedier underlife

Commute Time:

About 20 minutes

Physical Environment:

A small, privately owned, old-school strip joint on the avenue

Emotional Environment:

Oh, man. Complicated. A mix of love and hate.

I enjoy working in bars -- It's fast, fun, exciting and full of high drama. The music at Linda's was good, the DJ was great (and a really nice guy), and, strangely enough, one night I walked in and a friend from a former temp job was working the door. You never know who you'll meet at a strip club, and, a lot of the time, it isn't who you think it's going to be. The girls could be raunchy and fun, but they were often mentally unstable and most of the time I just felt bad for them. They seemed to give up so much and get so little back (in the form of real relationships or cash). Everyone at a strip club needs to be saved, in some fashion. And like any bar, there's room for introspection. As Henry Rollins says, "every now and again The God of Clubs smiles down and the night is just right, the crowd is just right, the music and dancers are spot on, and everyone has a great time." It's rare, though.

Nemeses:

I'm certain that Linda, herself, was one of the most frightening characters I've ever met. A *grande dame* who resembled a stout Elizabeth Taylor with a cane, she ruled with an iron fist, and not a whit of subtlety or humor. To work, you needed to look a certain way. That made sense, but she was harsh. "You look like shit. Go home." "Why are you wearing that?" "Don't you have anything shorter?" Or, my personal favorite, lobbed at me one night, "You ain't no Barbie, but you'll do. Now get to work." By the time she was done with me, the last thing I wanted was to do was serve drinks for six hours while wearing something that made me feel so incredibly vulnerable.

"What is that man drinking over there?"

"Uh, vodka and OJ."

"How many has he had?

"I'm not sure."

"Why are you not sure? Count his drinks, watch the clock, he needs to leave. He ain't buyin'. You go tell him to leave."

"Yes, ma'am."

It went on like this almost every night. I wanted to like her, as she was just another carnival character in her own freak show, but she made it really hard. On a good day, though, she would help a girl out with a new hair-do or a manicure by tossing money at her and telling her to go fix herself up. She was so heavy-handed and mercurial that I was very, very relieved when I quit.

Allies:

The customers weren't as bad as I'd imagined. Some were quite hot (I looked forward to seeing one in particular come in on a regular basis). Others were older, sad in some way, but very likeable. As a group, though, they could be picky and rude. As individuals, they were interesting, fun to talk and to flirt with.

Living Situation(s):

Alone in my own apartment rented from a property management company that kept sending The Sheriff over with nastygrams telling me to vacate within thirty days (due to my always-exciting job situation).

When I Knew:

I always knew, but I definitely knew the night that my bar back duties suddenly expanded to stagehand: "Girl, when you're done carrying down, go wipe the pole."

Departure:

Abrupt. I just left.

What I Think About When I Think About This Damn Job:

I remember staying up all night to clean and schlep the evening's empties down to the basement in a mini skirt. The birds singing as I finally got to put my head on my pillow, congratulating myself that I'd made it through another shift, and the $70 in my wallet that hadn't been there before. Sleeping some nights on huge bags of Styrofoam in the back of a friend's store and getting dressed and made up in the tiny mall bathroom before my shifts at Linda's. The love notes from law enforcement.

Theatre DayGlo

Employee:

FAXBoy

Location:

San Fiasco, California

Approximate Tenure:

Years(!) in the late 90s

Position Held:

Box Office Assistant and then Box Office Manager

AKA:

Jackass-in-a-Box

Elapsed Time Before Job Search Resumed:

I didn't look for another job because, at least initially, I was dodging some other more heinous graduate skool requirement by working here. Maybe this started as a paid internship (externship? sinkingship?) or something else bureaucratically ridiculous? I also didn't look because I was able to work nights and this jived perfectly with my lust for lager and howling at the moon.

Compensation:

$8.something/hour and then $10.something/hour after my promotion. (Come to think of it, this may have been my one, and only, promotion EVER(!))

Commute:

Totally on foot after falling out of my loft and stumbling out into the bright, bright Khalifournya sun. Once out onto Market Street, I was able to air out a little bit on my way to 16th and Mission. Unfortunately, I often ended up arriving at work in something of a rage after running the gauntlet of dealers and junkies by the BART station who always asked me if I was, "lookin', lookin'" and continually offered me "outfits, outfits" over and over and over again every g*d damn day. I started to yell at them because I felt like the only fucking guy in this particular neighborhood with an actual J-O-B (and that pissed me off to no end).

Commute Time:

Five-to-15 minutes, depending on the severity of my hangover and on my level of engagement with the local entrepreneurs

Physical Environment:

Somewhere between a bunker and a tree fort.

Theatre DayGlo was housed in a massive brick building that was home to other non-profits, galleries, and performance spaces, so the (tattered and sun-faded) Freak Flag waved proudly over this structure day and night.

Emotional Environment:

Wickedly familial, yet incredibly stressful

Nemeses:

Season ticket holders, anyone who ordered their tickets from The InterWeb (because they'd often show up to the wrong show at the wrong theatre on the wrong night and then yell at as because they missed *Cats*), and the junkies who did their damndest to rob us blind on a daily basis. Gary and Stanley, the platonic gay duo who had worked and volunteered together at this theatre for years and did what they did (and *only* did what they had done for years, no more, no less) when they weren't shopping for the second-hand and vintage clothing that they both wore. These clothes, you have to know, were originally designed and sized for children, so imagine two shoe-gazing hipster wannabes in their 30s (at least), with toxic 'tudes amplified by their surly solidarity, crammed into rainbow-colored Garanimals from the 70s who always seemed to be far too deep into conversation about the cultural significance of The Cure to take direction from me (or from anyone else).

Allies:

The Vietnamese family who ran the Pho joint across the street, the former Queen of the Box Office who trained me, and the lesbian artistic director who always clashed with her male counterpart, who liked to insert his latest one-man show into the season at the last minute when he thought that no one was looking.

Living Situation(s):

Chez Market Street with The Ex-Boyfriend, Sylvia Splash and her entourage, and The Marijuana Monster (who dealt a lot of drugs after dropping out of the same university).

When I Knew:

I think that I started numbering my own days when I got a desperate call to come in on a day off and I was still unmistakably wasted from the night/morning before. This didn't impede my job performance in the least, however, I was just embarrassed to let my queer colleagues witness the full extent of my personal messiness.

Departure:

Official and painful because, after it all, I liked this place and loved working with some of the people who bounced on and off of the payroll.

What I Think About When I Think About This Damn Job: That, at all times, someone had done somebody else wrong and everyone else had to know about it immediately. The touring production of Ronnie Larsen's *Ten Naked Men* that arrived, almost uninvited, like a plague of bitchy gay locusts that overstayed their welcome because people with clothes on really like to see other people without clothes on onstage (even if there is no plot or talent to be found under those bright lights). During rehearsals for this theatrical masterpiece, the porn stars and the strippers in the cast started fighting and there were actual brawls between the two nearly-naked factions out back. It was like some absurd *West Side Story* playing out backstage and then some of the strippers threatened to walk after some of the porn stars threatened to walk and none of us really knew if we'd have to change the marquis to read (*Approximately*) *Ten Naked Men* before opening night. Ronnie (the writer and director of this *magnum opus*) and his corpulent female business partner accused the box office staff of theft almost nightly after it did open, so I had to review the financials at the end of every shift until they would finally shut the fuck up and roll themselves into a bar somewhere to spend all of the money that we had just been arguing about. The junkies who would crawl into the building through sewer pipes to shoot up in our bathrooms and the arcs of dried blood that they left spattered across said bathroom walls from their hypodermic malfunctions. The fact that one of The Capp Street Girls (the one with the black teeth, pleated miniskirt, and fishnets who looked straight outta motherfuckin' *Slaves of New York*, I'm sure of it) stole the cheap clock from the dollar store off the dressing room wall one day. (The Capp Street Girls were the loose (haha!) band of prostitutes who worked the alley on the side of the building. These intrepid ladies worked 24/7 eight days a week and they looked it.) Being promised a production of my latest one-act and that, somehow, never happening. Working with theatre professionals who had names like "Trauma Flintstone" and SomethingSomething Cowboy. Catching a bike messenger's front tire in my crotch one night as I crossed 16th Street on my way to get dinner. The prickly mint leaves in the best spring rolls I've ever had in my life.

The San Francisco Skool for Incredibly Famous Artists of The Future

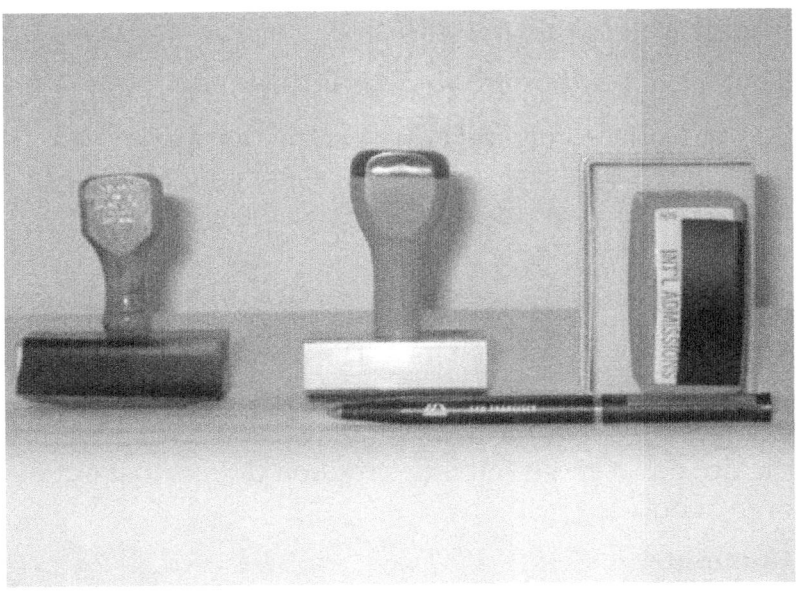

Employee:

FAXBoy

Location:

San Francisco, California

Approximate Tenure:

It had to be about three months or so in the summer of 1999 despite the fact that it felt like an eternity-and-a-half

Position Held:

International Admissions Administrative Assistant

AKA:

Stupid American Behind Desk

Elapsed Time Before Job Search Resumed:

At this point in my life, I don't know that I even had the wherewithal to even look for a job when I finally realized that I was dissatisfied with the one that I owned at the time.

Compensation:

$26,000.00/year -- WooHoo! (The same exact salary that I received working at Colossal Publishing Company #1, but this was before I worked for either of the dot coms and it felt like a million dollars just out of grad skool...)

Commute:

Anything that spilled down Market Street (bus, subway, surface train...) Typically, I hopped the F-Line in front of the crack hotel by FLAX and then dropped into the subway at Van Ness and popped above ground at Montgomery by The Palace Hotel (that I have since found out was once a Catholic orphanage). Sometimes, if I were sufficiently hung over and wanted to air out, I would walk.

Commute Time:

On mass transit, it took about 10 minutes. On foot, about 30.

Physical Environment:

Kinda neat because of the "artistic" atmosphere, but pretty much like any office hell anywhere that aspired to Modernism by way of shiny marble exteriors from the 80s with brushed metal elevators and sterile Lego-like desks and furnishings.

Emotional Environment:

Like detention all day long.

Nemeses:

All of the students from Korea, Japan, and China. Plus one horrible girl from Sweden.

Allies:

The OTHER gay guy in the office. He had worked in this office for years and years, had come and gone and come back again, and was looking to get out while I was employed at this fake university.

Living Situation(s):

Market Street with The Ex-Boyfriend, The Marijuana Monster, and The Freak? Craig? Jean-François? John? Sylvia Splash? It was Grand Central/Ellis Island of the West at the time.

When I Knew:

Almost immediately, but especially the first time that I went to slide the window across the front desk, so that I could go and take a piss and was informed, by like five people simultaneously, that The. Window. Is. Never. To. Be. Closed. During. Business. Hours. (People, apparently, had been fired on the spot by the president for this very infraction.)

The aforementioned "president" was actually just the great grand-daughter of the founder of the damn skool and they called her "The Queen of Hearts" because she would (essentially) walk around and scream, "Off with their heads!" at unsuspecting employees who were not floating her boat at that particular moment.

Departure:

Abrupt and passive (again). I went to "1984" at The Cat Club and drank and drank and danced and danced until somewhere between two and four in the morning. The other gay guy kept calling me in the days following because I left my ghetto blaster behind. It was Wendy's and it was old and it was covered in paint. (And I loved it, but it was an acceptable loss, though, considering...)

What I Think About When I Think About This Damn Job:

The incredibly high hopes that I had for the position itself as it was going to allow me to take classes (*à la* Super Wicked Old College). I had planned to rip through the screenwriting sequence and come out on the other side with a million-dollar contract. I did neither, unfortunately... The fact that EVERYONE'S "granfadda die" in Asia just before the Thanksgiving break and that all of these funerals were to be held in Cancun. (These students had to go through me to get their visas squared away by getting their I-9 forms stamped in triplicate. Years later I came across a group show at a gallery in New York called "I-9" and laughed at the in-joke despite my horrible experience at this particular "Famous Skool.")

This is the skool that produced those commercials that aired on MTV that Squishy and I would mock in the middle of the night, totally drunk, on the huge brown couch of her co-op. Salivating about becoming a published writer while staring at the Chronicle Books building out the window of my stupid office. Flying Tower Air (now defunct) to NYC for the weekend and being the last one on the return flight. (The door literally hit me in the ass!) The Omnipresent Fear of surprise termination at the hands of *Elle Presidente*...

IDon'tCareData.com

Employee:

FAXBoy

Location:

Silicon Alley, California

Approximate Tenure:

September 1999 – July 2000(-ish)

Position Held:

Editorial Analyst, eSearch Group

AKA:

Surfer, Dot Com Slacker

Elapsed Time Before Job Search Resumed:

None! N/A! I didn't look at all! I had just been removed from The San Francisco Skool for Incredibly Famous Artists of The Future (as if by The Jaws of Life), by Sylvia Splash (by way of The Bitch with Scissors) and I was so drunk that I didn't even think about employment (even on this job while I had it!) in any way, shape, or form. This was partially a product of the job itself as it didn't feel like work, most days, unless we were testing software before an update release.

Compensation:

Good, but I can't recall the exact dollar amount off the top of my head. At the time, it felt like millions upon millions of dot com dollars as there were stocks and options (stock options, even) and I thought, "Yeah... I totally faked my way into the easiest job on the planet."

Commute:

The beautiful and historic F-line down Market Street, subway from either the Van Ness or the Church Street station to either the Powell or the Montgomery Street station, plus a quick walk up Second Street to the weird coffee shack attached to the stubby office building. Everyone raved about this place (the weird coffee shack, not the stubby office building), but it resembled one of those fortuneteller machines from Ocean Beach or Coney Island except that this one was manned by a surly barista with magenta and canary-yellow hair who dispensed coffee that was just as inconsequential to life, liberty, and the pursuit of happiness as the predictions spewed from the aforementioned psychics in-a-box.

Commute Time:

10 or 15 minutes depending on the mood of the underground. MUNI never seemed to require its drivers to show up to work on a consistent basis and some of the subs would just burn the brakes up-and-down the main lines until some of the stations smelled like a house that had just been put out by The Fire Department.

Physical Environment:

Decent, if a bit fly-by-night, on the second floor of a small warehouse that was renovated in the 80s to house multiple businesses. I think that there were law firms and maybe some therapists in there with us, but we never saw them. We had most of the second floor after Microsoft lost interest in its Sidewalk.com venture and vacated an adjacent space. For some reason, this felt like a bloodless coup and there were several meetings in wide-open, and recently abandoned spaces that were painted in the Microsoft palette of the day. ("Sidewalk can't help anymore.") Our computers, however, were just set up on long folding tables that slowly started to buckle under the weight of the machines and from the pounding of their keyboards by a group of ham-handed Web monkeys.

Emotional Environment:

Sort of like being over at a friend's house in high school whose parents are overly permissive and slightly neurotic at the same time. Days and days would go by without much human interaction whatsoever and then there would be a flurry of activity and an attempt at accountability before the panic subsided and things returned to normal.

Nemeses:

Jeff? (Jack? John?) The gay engineer who, at first glance, was like the flannel-clad lumberjack of my dreams. Except that this studly woodsman actually lived at home with his mother and, for some reason, vehemently disliked me a couple of months into this particular gig. If there were data entry anomalies, he would assemble a malevolent posse at my desk to check my work and/or browser history. He seemed to resent that I did not live at home with my mother and the fact that I would often show up late to work, still drunk from the night before. (WTF?!?) Blane: My alleged boss, who I referred to as "Blannnnnnnnnd-uhhhhh" in conversation (pronounced as two long self-pitying syllables) because he was so boring. Blane was embroiled in the overly-protracted process of coming out to his wife and children as "bi" and filing for divorce at the same time and, for some reason, was under the false impression that this actually made him even remotely interesting. He lacked balls in such a serious way that sometimes it was difficult to talk to him. (Awk/ward!)

Allies:

Welcome Back Trotter -- An incredibly quiet guy who, it turns out, had led quite a wild existence before washing up on the shores of this odd medical software company. Funny as FUCK, a writer, and the man who introduced me to the music of Vic Chesnutt. If it weren't for this guy, I probably wouldn't have lasted half as long as I did.

Living Situation(s):

Chez Market Street with Sylvia Splash & Co., Lick + Riz, and The Marijuana Monster. Have I mentioned that The Marijuana Monster was incredibly short? And stoned 24/7 which made him smarter and taller than he really ever could be. I would often encounter him on the train in the morning as we were heading to our random temp jobs, bleary-eyed and redolent of *Eau de Bongwater.*

My favorite thing during these chance encounters was when he would be forced to jump what seemed like ten feet into the air in an attempt to catch one of the commuter straps when the train would inexplicably lurch to a sudden stop and he would just fall over. At those times, to quote Ms. Ross, "It took all the strength I had not to fall apart..." But I digress.

When I Knew: In the midst of one of those interminable "Where-Do-You-See-Yourself-In-Five-Years" one-on-one meetings with Blannnnnnnnd-uhhhhh at Café SomeThingorOther during the course of which I swear his hand grazed my thigh more than once underneath the tiny table. I think if I had replied: "In your bed" that I would have lasted just a little bit longer at this one, but I didn't. (Because he was Nast E.) I think he picked up lunch, though.

Departure: Instigated via conference call! (A first!) I was in my studio, painting up a storm for a show at another café in Hayes Valley, and the phone rang and it seemed like almost everyone in my office was on the line simultaneously. (They weren't, but there were some big wigs seated around a conference table calling (literally) for my prompt separation from the company.) Of course, they couldn't bring themselves to say this over the phone, so they kept asking me to come in (even though we had previously been given a half-day – WTF?!?) and I kept telling them that I was, uhh, busy painting up a storm and that I couldn't. Finally, I told them that I would be in at the end of the day (almost just to shut them up and to get them off of the f'n phone). I painted until five, having a couple of beers in the process, and hopped the subway and went back down to the office in order to accept the fact that I was most-certainly losing my job face-to-face with various managers who had so obviously failed to adequately manage me to their own exacting standards during our brief time together.

When I got up to the second floor, I was immediately whisked into the kitchen by the office manager who told me to act infinitely more upset than I actually felt while the deed was being done in order to secure my severance package. I hadn't thought of this because I had already gotten a job up the street at LookStupid.com and was on the verge of giving my notice before the whole firing thing went down anyway. After this debrief, I was ushered into a small conference room with a speakerphone module in the middle of the table and told that they were going to have to let me go, nothing personal, good luck in the future, if you need a reference let us know, "please." I attempted a countenance that projected an absurd amount of disappointment and pain, but instead maintained a sort of annoyed poker face and then made the rounds in the rest of the office, making a point to say (laboriously) how nice it was to work with each and every one of them. Then I waited around, a little awkwardly, for Blannnnnnnnd-uhhhhh. The office manager told me later (over drinks) that he was hiding in the bathroom the whole time. I like to imagine that he's living with Paul Bunion and his mother, dating them both to scratch the itch on both sides of his self-professed "complexity," and that they all share one huge Craftmatic.

What I Think About When I Think About This Damn Job:

Napster. Napster was essentially my job 75% of the time. Like, I would go to work and think, *"Now what was Tiffany's biggest hit?"* And then I'd go on a 7.5-hour journey through the pop diva's *oeuvre* that would, of course, lead me to the work of Samantha Fox, Apollonia, Vanity (of Vanity 6 fame), and then on into whatever became of the Mary Jane Girls. The pain and burning in my wrists and arms after a few weeks (from the repetitive stress) that brought me to tears on more than one occasion because I thought that I'd never write or paint ever again. Using bags of frozen peas to bring down this swelling.

Drunk girls wearing sequined cowboy hats over lime green wigs coating the streets of San Francisco with their Technicolor® vomit after a zillion-and-one self-congratulatory IPO parties. My fancy, yet worthless, souvenir placemat:

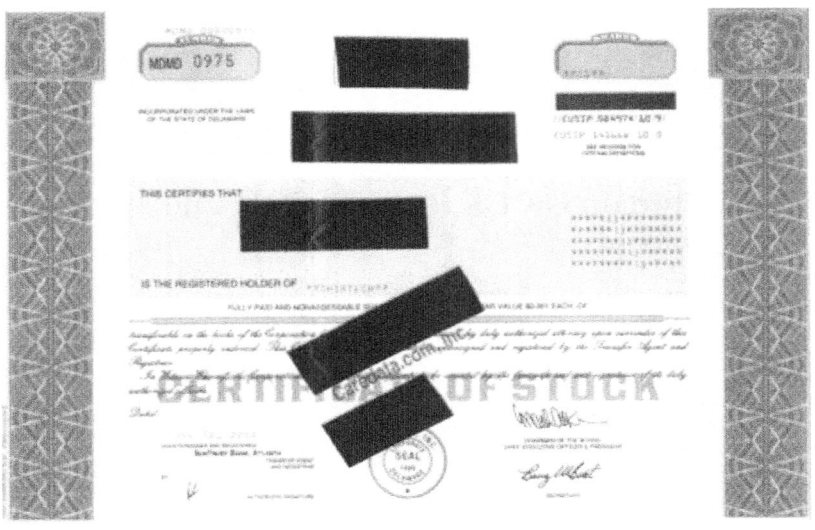

LookStupid.com

Employee:

FAXBoy

Location:

Silicon Alley, California

Approximate Tenure:

June 2000 - January 2001 AND April 2003 - January 2004

Position Held:

Health & Science Editor AND Small Business Listings Fulfillment Editor

AKA:

Surfer

Elapsed Time Before Job Search Resumed:

I actually didn't LOOK for another job. Until they fired me. (Twice.)

Compensation:

$36,000.00/year AND $38,500.00/year

Commute:

N-Judah from Van Ness (subway) to 2nd and King (surface)

Commute Time:

Thirty minutes

Physical Environment:

Stylish dot com enviro in the former "South End Warehouse." Beautiful brick building with *über* stylish interior: wide open spaces, exposed brick, original rusty factory doors, seismic I-beams throughout, glass conference rooms. All with that new car smell of hundreds of nerdy academic over-achievers elegantly arranged around a throbbing mainframe hidden (stylishly) somewhere in the building.

Emotional Environment:

Exactly like a library (a library without books, that is).

Nemeses:

The Economy AND The Business Development Team

Allies:

Skooter (BS, Biology, UC Berkeley), Snow (BA, English, Harvard), Welcome Back Trotter (MA, Philosophy, University of Texas at Austin).

Living Situation(s):

Market Street with The Ex-Boyfriend, The Bitch with Scissors, and The Marijuana Monster's Sister

When I Knew:

When I got the stupid e-mail(s). The first time, Skooter and I were working late on an Amazon.com project and a mass, templated message went out about a "special" meeting at 10:15 the following morning.

I had warned Skooter that I could feel it in the air and we were prepared (desks and hard drives were already cleaned and sanitized), but we took a tour of the building at about 8 o'clock the night before the first wave of layoffs and encountered a conference room full of Bigwigz drinking Heineken and laughing, laughing, laughing… The second time, I knew when I got the PERSONALIZED e-mail to come to ANOTHER special meeting with the same guy that officiated the first special meeting in 2001. I just kept repeating the word "motherfucker" over and over and over again as he read from his script.

Departure:

Raucous and rainy the first time. Slow and excruciating the second time.

What I Think About When I Think About This Damn Job:

How proud I was of myself (a rarity when thinking of my employment history, fo' sho'!) that I found this editorial job at LookStupid on Craig's List while I was still at IDon'tCareData.com at the other end of 2nd Street. I applied, walked back-and-forth a couple of times on my lunch hour for two interviews, and landed a swank new (higher paying) job that I wanted AND liked(!!!!!)

Keggers in the kitchen on Friday afternoons. Booking a trip to Vancouver on Travelocity (or Expedia) before that first Halloween. Going to see the Krystof Kozlowski trilogy at the UC Theatre in Berkeley with Skooter after we lost our jobs together. The fact that her first-generation Korean parents blamed her for this when she called them from my apartment where we were stripping off our wet clothes on either side of the heater in the front rooms. How she cried after she got off the phone. London. The Bay Bridge in the morning. Freighters in the harbor. Discovering Radiohead and David Gray. *Montréal* with FileGrrl (with Madonna's *Music* looping in the car on the drive up to the border). How stupid I feel that I went back. How stupid I feel that I got fired again. Being a total drunk mess the first time I worked here and then going back totally sober. Spending Christmas Eve in the office with my soon-to-be ex-boss, just the two of us, and how cloying the silence was.

Knights in Shining Hardware

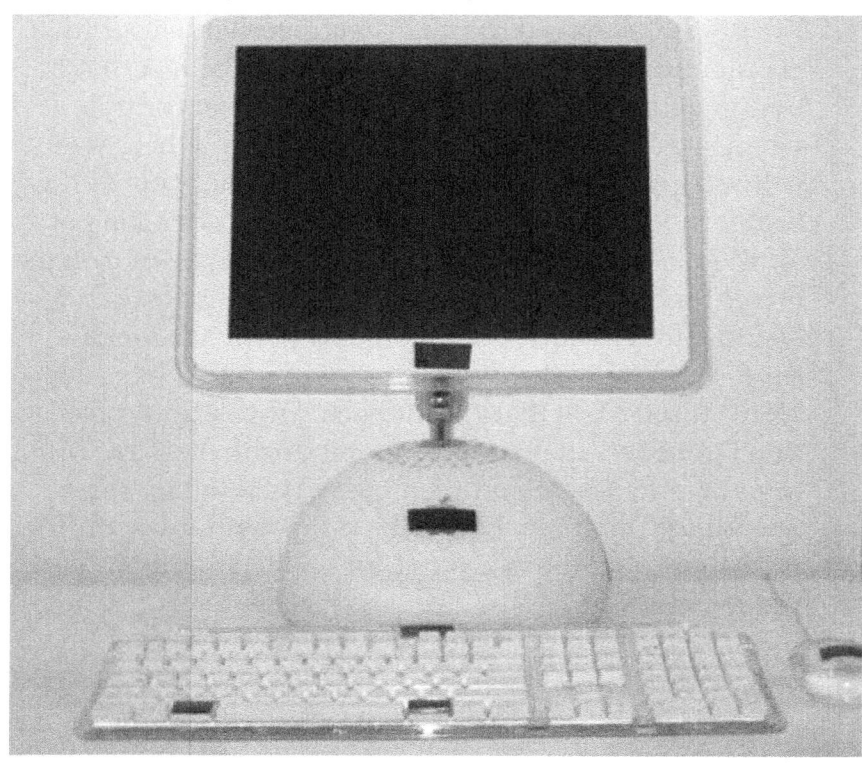

Employee:

FileGrrl

Location:

Latham, New York

Approximate Tenure:

October 2000 - December 2000

Position Held:

Sales Associate

AKA:

Receptionist/Administrative Assistant/Database Fornicator/Beeyatch for Owner

Elapsed Time Before Job Search Resumed:

Two days

Compensation:

$22k/year with additional ca$h after a six-month review (I didn't make it...)

Commute:

Back-and-forth on Route 7 thru the Latham Northway interchange bottleneck twice a day

Commute Time:

20+ minutes each way

Physical Environment:

Small, privately-owned building (well, by his mother) that had last been renovated sometime in the late 70s. Most of the windows were covered with classy used-car "BIG BLOW OUT"-sale-type signage.

Emotional Environment:

Sort of like sitting just outside the principal's office in elementary school after being kicked out of class for shooting spitballs. Or being on a malevolent version of *Gilligan's Island* where the castaways really, really hate you and won't tell you why they won't invite you to their stupid luau...

Nemeses:

Burt S., the supervising technician with the wildly mercurial personality (disorder, even). This was a man who presented a bottle cap (that he picked up from a gas station parking lot where he used to work) to his wife as an engagement ring. He enjoyed deploying really subtle (and not so subtle) put-downs of my intelligence, both in private where no one could hear him, and in public where others could enjoy the laughter at my expense. Ben Knight, the owner of ye olde computer shoppe. The allegedly helpful, yet totally paranoid, store manager who was convinced I was a spy for Someone Else. (For whom, exactly, I never quite figured out.)

Allies:

Dave, the gay superstar (and **brilliant** friend), who had been working for this company for five long years (even tho' it was always, always, always on the brink of disaster). He had been fired for numerous bizarre reasons, but was always rehired.

Living Situation(s):

With my then-fiancé. I was hired after said fiancé was fired from this very company and this exact position. Actually, they fired him, but then wanted him to be available to revise and troubleshoot various Web documents for this sorry store (for zero compensation), as if he were desperate for the URLs for his résumé (he wasn't).

About six months after firing him, they placed an ad in the paper for help. *Why did I answer?* I thought that, with coaching from my formerly-employed fiancé, I'd have a good shot at getting, and keeping, this one. I was wrong. While employed, he got along swimmingly with everyone, upgraded his own machines, and attended weekly LAN reindeer games. They helped him to become tech certified. Then they canned him. With me, they offered no such deals, interest, or education. I was their object of ridicule and they made fun of me after I couldn't tell a 12-pronged male plug from an 18-pronged example. It was only a matter of time. My imperfections were looming large. I'm certain that they were convinced that they were all intellectually superior to me. Mostly, they were just assholes. I hope that saying so is all pejorative and punitive and reflects badly on my soul for all kingdom come because, really, damn them to hell. I spent every moment at work reading hardware documents that I pulled from The Web. Except, and here's one of the biggest exceptions of my whole life: I'd not made enough money at that point to purchase a computer, therefore, I had NO idea how the systems worked, how to network them, or how to load them. My income hadn't allowed me to keep up with the technology and it was evident from day one. They initially said that they would train me, but without a computer to fiddle around with at home, I was dead in the water. They lost interest in me, I in them, and to make things worse, their sales were flatlining. Virtually no customers came into the store for anything other than quick repairs.

When I Knew:

The day that the Sales Manager went through my desk (and my Rolodex) looking for... something. Or maybe it was the day that that my boss was completely annoyed and confused by the basket of apples that I put on my desk (to display my enthusiasm for the hardware I supposed to be selling). Or maybe it was the day I brought in flavored coffee and found him gagging loudly while dumping out the entire freshly-brewed pot. (The office talked all morning about THAT!)

Departure:

Abrupt. Immediately after being told that "sales were down" and that they couldn't use me anymore. I packed everything on, and in, my desk (with glee) and was out the door in ten minutes flat! They were so paranoid, however, that they called me two days later and demanded my Rolodex. (I'd been scribbling names and numbers down to keep at my desk because they completely freaked out if I messed one up. I thought that creating my own back-up system showed initiative, but they didn't see it that way.) I'd taken said Rolodex with me because it was mine, but had tossed the used cards because, really, I could give a flying fuck if Dr. Smith might be interested in buying a printer three months from now. When I got the call that Mr. Knight wanted me to bring all of the cards back to him, I retrieved them from the garbage, shredded them by hand, and drove them back to the store. He wasn't in when I got there, but I carefully placed the bag of multicolored confetti in the center of his desk anyway.

What I Think About When I Think About This Damn Job:

Making the decision to never decorate my desk ever again. Not with fresh fruit, not with pretty pencils, nor with a Rolodex. Nothing. (What anyone provides me with is what I will do the job with.) And never to take a job with a company that can't afford the odd stapler or a three-hole-punch. Learning, once and for all, how to take a damn fine phone message by assuming that the recipient has no idea who his lawyer, accountant, mother, or wife is or what their names or numbers might be. The poor, grossly overweight fellow at the Kwik-E-Mart down the street who'd wrap up my Reuben each day and say, while handing it over the counter and drooling (at me or at his sublime sandwich artistry, I'll never know), "That will make a tasty morsel." Taking the dripping hot, sauerkraut-infused thing out by the airport to watch jets take off for better places. The fall becoming colder, but refusing to eat at my desk because of the claustrophobic atmosphere in the office. My delightful severance check. Never forgiving them for taking me from a job I'd been at for almost three years only to dump me after two months into the gaping maw of the failed dot com and computer industries. *Montréal* at night...

Transcribers 'R Us!

Employee:

FAXBoy

Location:

Berzerkeley, California

Approximate Tenure:

April Something, 2001 - June Something, 2001 (This is the first crap job that I jumped at after I got back from *Montréal*…)

Position Held:

Editorial Assistant. I was hired to transcribe interviews with prominent members of local biotechnology companies from fuzzy audiocassettes into Microsoft Worst for eight hours a day. ALL of these prominent men and women had incomprehensible German accents and pronounced speech impediments.

AKA:

Angry Monkey Strapped to Desk

Elapsed Time Before Job Search Resumed:

About a month

Compensation:

In between $30k and $32k/year

Commute:

I FAXed myself from the Civic Centre to the Downtown Berzerkeley station on BART and then scrambled up the hill through downtown Berzerkeley, and the lower campus of UC Berkeley, to the office.

Commute Time:

40+ minutes each way

Physical Environment:

The upper floor of a gorgeous old library in the center of campus that was all brass and marble and musty in that intoxicatingly academic way.

Emotional Environment:

Exactly like detention. Or what I image it would feel like to be a hostage.

Nemeses:

The Beige Brigade (a battalion of women who seemed to cut their bangs with safety scissors and throw their ragged souls in the dryer at the end of the day to further blanche their personalities, i.e., EVERYONE I worked "with," but most especially BeckyBeckyPh.D.) BBPh.D. resembled a green bean left on a windowsill for a year or so and she was such a MISERABLE bitch. She had a head of wiry untamed salt-and-pepper corkscrews that made her even uglier to the point that I had to turn away every time she approached lest I turn to stone.

Allies:

None. One fake friend.

Living Situation(s):

Market Street with The Ex-Boyfriend (and maybe The Bitch with Scissors)

When I Knew:

When they moved me, for no apparent reason, from the office with the windows to the office in the middle of the building. Rules of This Particular Captivity: No natural light, no food, no coffee, no personal phone calls, no unauthorized use of the Internet, no fun, no smiling, and no men. I DEFINITELY KNEW the day that I was working on my résumé and I accidentally sent it, with a stunning cover letter, to the main office across the hall to print. The Beige Brigade had a field day with that one.

Departure:

Abrupt. Pseudo blaze of glory. Wuz desperately seeking other employment in my cube-in-a-cave when, all of a sudden, the Beige Brigade was standing behind me in a semicircle with their arms folded and frowns all around. BBPh.D. informed me that "we" were weeks behind on this particular project and "What was taking me so long?" I found out that I was being paid on a per-project basis from grants that they received for each particular project (uhh, didn't know that) and that they were billing my hours against these individual grants. (All of this despite the fact that I was getting the same paycheck every two weeks. I honestly had no idea how my ass wuz funded and didn't really care, either…)

So, I stalled for time and yapped about the clarity of the tapes and about the accents straight out *auf* motherfuckin' *Deutschland*, but they weren't buying it and I was summarily ADMINISTRATED about NOT using the Web to job hunt or to communicate with the world outside. I think they set up a meeting for later in the day, but I took a lap around downtown Berkeley and fumed. I returned to my desk and wiped my files, popped Joni Mitchell's *Court and Spark* out of my Dictaphone, walked into the office, pulled my fake ham sandwiches out of the mini-fridge, and told them "Not to bill my hours for June" or some such thing that indicated that I was quitting at that very moment. And I did. I took the subway back home and then carted 6,000lbs of dirty laundry across the street and was hit by a tweaker flying down Market Street on a stunt bike and was so OVER just about everything that I walked away from him as he pounded his chest and called me "bitch" over and over. **Bring. It.** Was the mood that I was in... The Ex-Boyfriend was very nice and quite understanding when he found me at the Laundromat later in the evening (thank g*d).

What I Think of When I Think of This Damn Job:

Sitting in front of the Campanile, staring up at the bust of Lincoln (who stared back) while sitting on the stone bench engraved with the following: "BENEFICIARY TO BENEFACTOR CLASS OF 1955" listening to the bells chime at 8AM and the distant sounds of trains departing from Amtrak in Emeryville.

Sitting in the wooden phone booths on the first floor of the library while searching for another job, The Wall Berlin off of Telegraph (pseudo-punk rock coffee *haus* where I spent most of my time and all of my money), the BART trains bobbing up and down from the tunnel to the surface like a metallic Loch Ness monster, the barbed wire that decorated the chain link fence on the side of the tracks, the easels and the pup tents inside the big blue warehouse full of artists (see entry for Weird Bank) seen from said train on the way to-and-from work. The day that my Fake Friend took me to The Free Speech Café (across from the library) and we sat out on the patio and I looked at the building across the way that had the names of various academic disciplines engraved around the cornice and how Zoology (the middle vowels overlapped) and Biochemistry (the 'o' and the 'c' overlapped) made me think of Led Zeppelin, and how the first thing out of her mouth was, "You hate your job, don't you?" I replied in the affirmative and she just went off, too, about how she hated her job, hated Berzerkeley (the university), and hated her husband for making them buy a house in Berzerkely (the city), and on and on and on… And then she listed the things that she did in the morning in order to put off going to work. My Fake Friend had a face like a Shar-Pei. Finding a copy of *Generation X* at the bookstore on the first floor for $4 and taking that as a sign that everything would be OK. Receiving some sort of tax document from Transcribers 'R Us! months after my departure that listed my tenure in this position as something like: **.186 years**. (Which was exactly .186 years too long.)

Information Superhighway

Employee:

FileGrrl

Location:

Albany, New York

Approximate Tenure:

June 2001 - Dec. 2001

Position Held:

Help Desk Intern

AKA:

New Girl

Elapsed Time Before Job Search Resumed:

Six months

Compensation:

$10/hour

Commute:

A few frigid minutes in a car with no heat to a large parking lot just off of The Information Superhighway. Easy!

Commute Time:

25 minutes (max)

Physical Environment:

In the basement of a Cold War building with air raid signs still attached. *Rad*! Sequestered in the bowels of this building next to the janitor's closet, I did not have my own cube or machine, although a machine was always readily available to log into to check current job tickets.

Emotional Environment:

It varied. Some days were easy, fun even, and others were nightmarish. Despite these highs and lows, I really liked this job.

Nemeses:

Leena, Leena Help Desk Diva -- Leena was beautiful, in a very Eastern-Euro-meets-New-York-City kind of way. She spent most of the day rummaging through her cosmetics bag and gazing intently into her compact mirror in order to keep her face in top shape while she was on the phone. She was engaging and personable in a superficial kind of way, until she'd accumulated enough dirt on you to start the machinations. She was socially manipulative in the most professionally malevolent fashion which, in my estimation, meant that she was adept at turning any given situation into a lose-lose proposition for you, no matter what you said. In short, I learned to hate her. (Ultimately, I didn't even want to be liked by her. In fact, I wanted her as far away from me as possible.) She finally just stopped talking to me altogether and I was glad because, except for the added tension in the air, her silence was a spectacular bonus.

Ever the pro manipulator, even though she wasn't talking to me, she continued to mess with my job (even though she was a secretary, essentially). So when a call came through that someone in the building needed their machine looked at, she'd glare at me, then look around the rest of the room and tell them that "no one was available to help them at the moment, but that as soon as one of the guys came back, she'd be sure to send them right out." There was no way for me to retaliate. I couldn't talk to her, as she was dead to me (*DEAD, I tell you!*), and she'd already stopped acknowledging me. I couldn't go to our boss, as she would have figured out a way to make my life even worse. She was evil, vicious, ignorant, and yet… amazing. May she rot in hell.

Allies:

Hank. Hank was mostly silent and very stoic. As a Native American, he spoke in one-or-two word sentences that conveyed a lot of meaning and wasted little breath. He understood The Help Desk Diva and said that life became easier when she stopped speaking to you. He found something redeeming in me, took me under his wing, nurtured my curiosity about the machines we worked on, told me when not to worry about things, and advised me to use fewer words. Hank was a very wise man.

Living Situation(s):

With my soon-to-be-ex-fiancé in a brownstone where the landlord lived downstairs from us.

He not only hated me, but would really only speak to the fiancé as if I were invisible. (I once had a whole conversation with him as he bent over fixing something. It was just the two of us in a room and as I was rounding off sentence number three (of what I thought was friendly chatter), he slowly turned to me and asked, "Are you speaking to me?" Mortified, I could only answer in the negative, "I guess not." The apartment itself was jam-packed with my soon-to-be-ex's collectibles, while my own things were relegated to boxes in dark corners. We both refused to part with the sofas that we rode in on, making the set-up feel even more temporary than it already did. The whole arrangement really didn't work for me on any level or for very long.

When I Knew:

When I failed my math exam. Technically, this was an internship that was somehow connected to the math and technology departments at the local community college.

To obtain the position, you had to be enrolled in at least one three-credit math course, or some such thing, and one's grades could not dip below 2.5 or 3.0 or some number that I obviously didn't meet. And, unfortunately, I'd signed myself up for a math class that was way too advanced for me and I failed it spectacularly. So, I lost my dreamy help desk job and spent an entire night walking aimlessly across the huge campus sobbing to myself. There was no recourse. I felt like an abject failure. Period.

Departure:

Slow, grinding, tortuous. I wanted to stay; yet, I could not.

What I Think About When I Think About This Damn Job:

I cannot think of this job without thinking of 9/11, pain, and death. My boss running past me and Hank, shouting, "Get back to the basement! We need ALL of you! The whole world has just gone to hell-in-a-hand-basket!" E-mailing FAXBoy to see if everyone in New York City was OK (or if he'd even heard about the attacks out in San Francisco). The door (literally) falling off of my car and having to hold it in place with one hand as I drove around looking for a garage that would bolt it back on. Leaving my fiancé. Losing my beloved leather jacket. (*Was it stolen? Burned in effigy by the ex-fiancé?* I'll never know.) Having the heater in the car quit in the dead of winter the same week that I got the flu. That, every now and then, there are low periods in life, where all of your plans fall through and everything gets dark and precarious. That I wanted to learn more, to be more useful, to create some fantasy of this help desk job where all I had to do was run around and perform software miracles, cure digital ills, eat a quiet lunch with Hank every day, and get paid for it.

The San Francisco Skool for Incredibly Famous Musicians of The Future

Employee:

FAXBoy

Location:

I will give you one guess…

Approximate Tenure:

June 2001 - September 2001

Position Held:

Development Assistant

AKA:

Receptionist/Administrative Assistant/Database Administrator/Beeyatch for VP

Elapsed Time Before Job Search Resumed:

Two days

Compensation:

$30k/year with an additional $1k after brief probationary period (I didn't make it...)

Commute:

N-Judah (surface, reverse commute) from Church St. to 19th Avenue and then six blocks on foot to 19th and Ortega

Commute Time:

30+ minutes each way

Physical Environment:

Small wooden structure behind Mission-style main hall that served as the "medical arts" building for the original orphanage founded circa 1903. (The strange vestigial hardware in the bathroom made gruesome sense after this revelation.)

Emotional Environment:

Worse than spending eight-to-ten hours in a high-school locker

Nemeses:

The Vice President of Development (the Jekyll-and-Hyde overseer) and Kay SomethingOrOther, a bitch on crutches w/huge, nasty hair

Allies:

Carrie OnMyWayWardSon, veteran admin of six-to-twelve months and seasoned VP Hater

Living Situation(s):

On Market with The Ex-Boyfriend

When I Knew:

The day I was ripped a new asshole for notating a concurrent meeting in The VP's appointment book. ("Are you *that* stupid? How can I be in two meetings AT THE SAME TIME?") Some other bigwig had made the request that I note the second meeting in the damn book...

Departure:

Abrupt. Immediately after being handed my final "live" check at the end of my exit interview (roughly 12:30PST), I hit the road and caught the next train home.

What I Think About When I Think About This Damn Job:

The smell of incense burning in the shrines of Chinese restaurants and shops, Vegetable DeLuxe for $3.50 @ Little Beijing, the smell of The Goal Post (a hardcore Irish drinking establishment) and the sound of the drunks and the television coming from the bar on my way to work, sporadic piano concertos and random outbursts from fledgling string quartets, walking unexpectedly through the needle exchange behind Safeway after I got off of the N and the Buddhist monk handing hypodermics and oranges to the assembled junkies as my legs turned to jelly beneath me on that last day.

Colossal Publishing Company #2

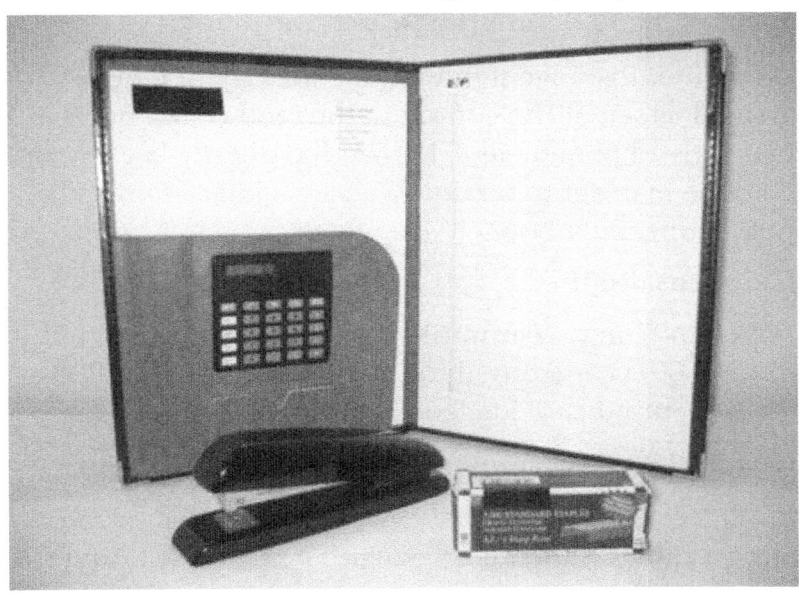

Employee:

FAXBoy

Location:

San Francisco, California

Approximate Tenure:

September 7th, 2001 (the Friday before 9/11) – February 3rd, 2003

Position Held:

Editorial Assistant

AKA:

Indentured Publishing Servant/Volunteer

Elapsed Time Before Job Search Resumed:

Three months. I went in with the idea that I had arrived, albeit at the bottom of the food chain, but that I had arrived nonetheless. I vowed to dig my heels in on day one in order to become a success in academic publishing. Silly boy…

Compensation:

$24ksomething/year until I got a raise to $25,999.00/year (roughly $12k less than I was making at LookStupid.com just before the first layoff)

Commute:

F-Market (surface) almost door-to-door to Pier 23 or Subway to F-Market (surface) at The Ferry Building or Subway to Sansome Street and thirteen blocks on foot (above ground:-)

Commute Time:

45 minutes or 25 minutes or 30-ish minutes

Physical Environment: Converted popcorn factory in a neighborhood of old brick warehouses. Stunning in retrospect, actually, but the whole surrounding area had been given that austere office park sorta facelift (courtesy of the Levi's headquarters next door). You know, opaque black windows and manicured, manicured, manicured everything else (people, plants, sidewalks…)

The interior of the office was something like Orwell-meets-Alcatraz-Island with a ton of exposed concrete, wiring, pipes, and fluorescent lighting angled this way and that for maximum dramatic effect. The second floor ceiling was actually up on the third floor and there was a catwalk/shooting gallery around the third floor that allowed people to literally walk around the top of my cube and read the text of the personal e-mail that was invariably flickering on my screen.

Emotional Environment:

Cold and precocious, but relatively professional. All of the publishing matrons had that TimeClock Martyr Syndrome ("I was here until *three* in the morning and we ran out of toner, so I ground some black pigment from a batch of old diskettes that I found in the basement, blah, blah, blah...") like they wanted to be blindfolded, strapped to one of the load-bearing columns with some UPS packing tape, and shot full of No. 2 pencils from a distance.

Nemeses: Fucking Phil, Scary Harry, and The Porn Star (Codename: *L'Etoile*). Scary Harry showed up late in the game AS A TEMP and then decided that he was my boss. (He had been working in publishing for years and years and years, but no one would have him back at this point because he was so ANNOYING). Fucking Phil was the totally homophobic, misogynistic, raging alcoholic Vice President that I had some NASTY exchanges with.

For instance: He barked some inane orders at me on a Wednesday and told me to have a project to him by the following Tuesday. I finished it on Monday and then ended up in the dentist's chair on said Tuesday morning. He FLIPPED the fuck out and roared through the office calling for my head. He had people call my house, The Ex-Boyfriend, and my friend, Welcome Back Trotter, who worked there as a temp before being reabsorbed into the completely dysfunctional LookStupid family. As soon as I stepped on to the floor, I knew there was a problem, so I dropped the twenty-or-so pages of info on his desk and said something to the effect of: "You said 'by Tuesday.' Here it is. And, oh, by the way... It's Tuesday." He super mega did not like getting bitch slapped by an EA and we never got along from that moment on. Oh, yeah. On Welcome Back Trotter's last day, he announced to the assembled employees that his cake (which, admittedly, was a nice gesture), "Shouldn't be fucking pink." The asshole was from Boston and if he weren't still there, I'd actually think about reapplying someday. The Porn Star pretty much trained me, so every time I fucked up I was like, "Well, Ashleigh (or however the hell you spell it) told me to do it that way." Meanwhile, The St*r cultivated an ever-shrinking wardrobe from GapKidz and Ralph Lauren PrePube (plunging necklines, midriffs, and low riders 24/7). She used any excuse to bend over and expose the stupid sun tattoo over her ass AND IT WORKED. Fucking Phil promoted her based solely on her Southern accent and blinding flesh headlights. At first I didn't really care, but then she started acting like my boss and I was like, "Hey! I have thirteen bosses and I'm the only one who's actually working..."

This I did not like and I voiced these thoughts to my new boss after I was passed around like a joint at Phish show. My opening line, once the stylish glass-and-wooden door was closed, was that "I [did] not want to be Assleigh's beyatch anymore!" I went on for, like, two hours about that little harlot... Ooops.

Allies:

Thelma and Louise, two of the awesomest people I have ever worked with/or for. (Louise took me to Houston's on her last day.)*

Living Situation(s):

On Market Street with The Ex-Boyfriend (and possibly Ted?)

When I Knew:

The first time *L'Etoile* stole credit for a project that I busted my ass on, but really after Thelma and Louise jumped ship because of Fucking Phil.

Departure:

Official, actually. I gave two week's notice, possibly three, I'm not sure. Wuz starting at Weird Bank & Distrust after the first of the year, so I decided to play nice. Plus, I liked the guy that inherited me. He swore a lot.

What I Think About When I Think About This Damn Job: Science!, standing at the copy machine by the sink under the catwalk in the dark for hours and hours and hours while lamenting the whole grad skool thing entirely, working with The Mathematician on a CD-ROM about cell structure, deadlines like never before, killing time at the end by walking out to the end of Pier 5 where most of the city sounds couldn't reach (except for the gulls and the ferries and the muffled traffic on The Bay Bridge), working late nights and off hours and writing that article about sleep deprivation for Salon.com in a blaze of caffeinated glory one night (that they rejected), the soy lattés at *Il Fornaio*, knowing enough to take the stapler this time around, and the squawk of the wild green parrots who live in the trees outside the building.

* This is where BritKnee took me on my first day when I started "working" at Colossal Publishing Company #1.

Color Me Annoyed

Employee:

FileGrrl

Location:

Albany, New York

Approximate Tenure:

Two months from February of 2002 through April of 2002

Position Held:

Ceramics Assistant

AKA:

Waitress/Chore Girl

Elapsed Time Before Job Search Resumed:

Two months

Compensation:

$8.50/hour

Commute:

In a car with no shock absorbers, a nearly-split back axle, and no heat through most of a miserable winter in Upstate New York. Chilly. But at least the tape deck worked.

Commute Time:

15 minutes

Physical Environment:

Grand ballroom of a pottery studio and everything you'd expect to find in a chic, hip, baby-boomer infested upscale strip mall: Cute tool holders on each table, a dark grey utilitarian concrete floor, an entire wall filled with adorable and sophisticated shapes to paint, and a revolving door of upscale, smart wives-of-lawyers with far too much time on their hands, ready to paint. Adorable!

Emotional Environment:

Seventh fiddle in a room full of creative, angry women. There was no outlet for creativity as an employee, however, unless you'd worked your way up the ranks to being second or first fiddle in this particular orchestra. The women I worked with were intelligent, sarcastic, biting, and (sometimes) even helpful. But they made it abundantly clear that I was the lowest on the totem pole.

Assignments would be doled out according to rank and, as lowest woman on the pole, I was allowed to hold sandpaper and rub out imperfections in the bisque. ("Don't call it "'greenware!'" For some reason, it was not "greenware.") I was allowed to wipe up paint spills and clean the toilet (as I'm always good for that). But emptying the kiln was reserved for much more functional chore girls. Dremeling® out imperfections required special permission to use the electric Dremel® tool. I never earned the right to Dremel®. (Years later, I asked for a Dremel® for Christmas so I could Dremel® my little heart out. No one could figure out why I wanted a Dremel® so terribly or why I still enjoy making holes in things.)

Nemeses:

The owner who worked alongside us every single day. Every Single Day. And her investment-banker husband, a kind and gentle soul whom I came to think of as a spy for some reason.

Allies:

Stephanie, The Fairy Princess. Trina "Why Was I Hired?" McCoy. We'd rub out imperfections in unfired clay vases together as if our very lives depended on it.

Living Situation(s):

About to be evicted from a very sweet apartment as I continued to live on the edge of about-to-be-homeless. Very often, food came from friends. The apartment itself was rented from my former brother-in-law and the sun streamed in in copious amounts, I had access to an attic that allowed me to get organized for the first time in years, and there was even office space (but no computer). (There was, however, a hungry kitten to feed.) Mail, including paychecks from temp agencies, was stolen from my box on a regular basis.

When I Knew:

When the owner stopped looking me in the eyes. Then one day she whisked me up the stairs (spiral, cast iron) to her office (cramped, jam packed with artist literature and shipments) to tell me that I "just wasn't what she was looking for." After two months? Thanks for that!

Departure:

Abrupt. I trod back down the spiral, iron staircase, turned in my apron, and walked out into the sun.

What I Think About When I Think About This Damn Job:

The smell of bread from the bakery next door mixing with the odd smells of the kilns. How warm the back room was in February. My ugly apron covered in glaze. Spoiled rotten brats named "Viktoria" and "Britney" and "Courtney" having ultra-well heeled birthday parties and their nasty, nasty mothers who forked over large chunks of change for the privilege of having drippy bears, seals, and heart-shaped boxes painted by their little darlings. Wiping frosting off the floor after the fact. Cleaning the toilet. (Again and again.) Being treated like I was the quaint, hired help by the customers -- "Look! She's artsy!" (And worse.) My absolute jealousy over the women I worked with who took yoga classes together, went to Paris together, were in Master's programs in art, etc., etc, etc... all the while crying poverty(!) Calling FAXBoy (at his post at The San Francisco Skool for Incredibly Famous Artists of The Future on the 800 #) from the payphone outside to keep my sanity. Then one day that payphone disappeared and was replaced with... nothing.

Wretched Wireless

Employee:

FileGrrl

Location:

Latham, New York

Approximate Tenure:

January 2002 - February 2002

Position Held:

Programmer

AKA:

Telephone Operator/Whipping Girl

Elapsed Time Before Job Search Resumed:

Thirty seconds

Compensation:

No recollection

Commute:

No recollection, but it definitely involved the freezing cold...

Commute Time:

Half-hour, each way

Physical Environment:

Transitional: Large warehouse full of computers and monitors. Individual cubbyholes with each cube's desktop chopped slightly too short to truly fit the monitor, the keyboard, and the coffee mug that were required to do one's job (requiring the keyboards to often rest in our laps in order to change position). The last business that occupied the space looked like they'd never fully moved out and the current business didn't look like they were too sure about staying in the space, either.

Emotional Environment:

Much like that of a hog on a hog farm, I imagine...

Nemeses:

The Clock. Slimy Steve from Ohio who would call and ask how long I'd been employed and could I do him a favor and please give him a supervisor? Every. Time. He. Called.

Allies:

Kathy, one of my sister's friends and the former resident of my then-apartment, whom I made every attempt to befriend by bringing her her unforwarded mail and other forgotten household belongings.

I did this until my sister explained to me that they really weren't all that close and to just let her wallow in her own misery.

Living Situation(s):

Squatting in Kathy's former apartment (see above) that was owned by my sister and my then-brother-in-law. I'm pretty sure that I still owe them about a grand for that apartment. (*But now that they're working on a divorce, should I split that payment up?*) My fiancé would bring me scratch-offs to see if I could rub off enough cash for a sub for dinner or gas to get back to work the next day. Some days he'd just bring me winning scratch-offs and sometimes he'd simply hand me cash.

When I Knew:

When I came down with the flu and spent three days tucked in bed with mass quantities of ginger ale and Tylenol®, instead of taking orders for crappy pager plans, and I was told that they needed a "doctor's order" if I was "that sick." Y'know, sometimes you're "that sick" and there isn't really a doctor available for the amount of money you're making. Or maybe it was the day my boss was pulled aside by her boss to speak to me about the fact that I was eating my lunch at my desk, an infraction I never comprehended, especially since the conversation and the atmosphere in the lunchroom were so cheery. (They were "expanding": knocking out one wall while plastic sheeting, hanging from the recently-exposed beams, concealed the other half of the room. Thus, one needed to clear off the plaster dust from the construction (and the grease from the table) with the used napkins from the hogs who had just eaten at the same trough before you could even sit down. People were young enough to mostly be living at home, which made my measly peanut-butter-on-wheat totally pale in comparison to their extravagant take-out lunches involving garlic bread, soup, rolls, pizza, subs, Chinese, and St*rfux® afforded by their completely disposable incomes.) Being administrated *again* for "reading on the job" after I brought in business and sales books to occupy my brain in between calls. I was told that I was "loafing" and being "inappropriate." Dumbasses. No wonder they're out of business now.

Departure:

Abrupt. Found another job ASAP and went back to pick up my box of personal belongings from a boss who told me they just "weren't satisfied with my performance." I wasn't all that satisfied with theirs either, so we were even.

What I Think About When I Think About This Damn Job:

My emergency box of dehydrated milk hidden in the pantry. My friends leaving groceries outside of my door and then running away so they wouldn't catch my flu or my poverty. The heater in my car failing to work. The parking lot (a loose collection of mud and large stones) that one could only use if one had been with the company for a year or more, as if such a non-privilege would earn long-term employee loyalty. My fiancé nursing me back to health with aspirin, cough suppressants, and tea. The local Fire Department driving me home because the drugstore lady wouldn't let me get behind the wheel after I nearly passed out while she was ringing up my Ensure®. The staggering youth of the average hog in this particular hog pen. That we all got free pagers, for some reason, a benefit made particularly enticing by the fact that most of us already owned cell phones. The *miserable* sales people in Ohio. Trying to sleep through it all.

That Truck Routing Place

Employee:

FileGrrl

Location:

Albany, New York

Approximate Tenure:

One month from August 2001 to September 2001

Position Held:

Online Router for Commercial Truckers

AKA:

That Stupid Bitch

Elapsed Time Before Job Search Resumed:

One month

Compensation:

I suppose there was money involved.

Commute:

Running down Western Avenue on foot, cutting up Quail Street, then barreling full-tilt down Central Avenue past The Job Corps office where the drunks (still drunk from the night before and crawling out of their live-ins at Pauly's Hotel and The Saloon) were ready to greet me as I made a mad lunge for the door, for the final sprint up the steps to my desk by 7AM.

Commute Time:

30 minutes

Physical Environment:

Stuck in a really, really bad, ugly student apartment where the landlord had apparently died, but no one from his immediate family was aware that he'd owned any property, so it just sat, melting and sagging like a clock in a painting by Dalí, for years. This tenement was filled to the max with desks that provided a sort of strung-out visual history of office furniture through the ages, starting in the 1950s with solid oak and landing squarely in the 80s with nasty pressed wood. If they could have chained us to this furniture, they would have. If you got up to leave your desk for any reason, they looked at you like you were a newly-escaped convict hanging from the razor wire and then they would ask if they "could help you." We were supposed to be assisting commercial truckers loaded down with crap to get from one end of a map to the other using nothing but their proprietary software. I received about five minutes of training about how to get a semi from say, Buffalo, New York, to Bangor, Maine, and then was left to fend for myself. Technically, I could direct questions to my supervisor who sat behind me, but he was usually on the phone with The Big Boss or with a client. Which meant I could wait for over a half-hour for an order to be put through while I tried to figure out the next leg of a trip for a place on a map I'd never heard of in my life.

I know that truckers from Lake Michigan to Massapequa were cursing the very ground I walked on. And I spent a lot of time praying that they wouldn't get pulled over hauling logs (or a doublewide mobile home) on a no-access road that I may have inadvertently sent them down. It just sucked.

I am almost certain that there is a trailer still running across the width of Pennsylvania searching for an exit that never existed.

Emotional Environment:

Mission: Impossible. Get the trucker across the border. Pray the police are sleeping. Pray you did it right. Pray that a really, really pissed off client didn't call The Big Boss with your dispatch number. Pray that you'd get it better tomorrow; pray that you got it right today. Essentially, I just prayed that the sins from one day wouldn't be too bad to keep me from coming back the next day. Added to this was the fact that my bottom left-hand drawer was filled with the personal effects of the girl who sat at the desk just before me. Contents included: Photos of her and her boyfriend with their dog, a coffee mug, Tampax®, Tupperware®, a fork, and a stale snack in a bag. It was like going spelunking and finding the prior explorer's bones preserved in a latticework of cobwebs. Even better: They made me box it all up after three weeks to bring down to Bobbie Sue when she finally came back to collect it all. *Quelle horreur*!!

Nemeses:

The FAX machine and the pregnant teenager who sat next to it. Our orders would come in over the wires and sometimes we were backed up all morning with companies waiting for directions, which was good because it meant we were busy and bad because it meant we were behind.

And sometimes orders came through so slowly that, as soon as the girl-in-a-family-way who babysat the machine was done with her first routing, she could just grab another order, which was bad because it meant that I didn't get any work. And if there wasn't any work, you got let go (which is exactly how this story ends).

Allies:

My immediate supervisor, a big teddy bear of a guy, who actually seemed to like (and to feel sorry for) me.

Living Situation(s):

With a man who I was engaged to (the same one who scratched off the winning LOTTO tickets to feed me). I mean, true love, right? In a student apartment with a sweeping veranda and large, Southern-style rooms. Except that the other kids who lived in the building were half my age and 10X as drunk and stoned as I've ever been, considering that I'm sober most of the time, which is to say that when the catfights between dueling Britneys erupt at 3AM ("I fucking HATE you, BITCH! I will NEVER talk to you EVER. FUCKING. AGAIN!!"), I'd often be one of the mean ladies on the phone with the police.

When I Knew:

When I returned from my cousin's wedding and listened to the "You're fired!" message on the answering machine. This was a temp-to-perm job. This is when I learned that all "temp-to-perm" really means is "we keep you until we don't need you or we deem you to suck for any reason" (i.e., it means nothing).

Departure:

Abrupt. I walked in and told my supervisor (he didn't know as The Big Boss hadn't informed him of my termination), threw my coffee mug and a few CDs into my backpack, gave him a hug, and then hit the street. I was a free woman by 8AM.

What I Think About When I Think About This Damn Job:

The gauntlet of drunks every morning. How filthy the conditions were. Being bored silly. Fighting an unspoken, losing battle with a pregnant woman for paperwork. How happy I was to leave.

Strive House

Employee:

FileGrrl

Location:

Albany, New York

Approximate Tenure:

Forever-and-a-day 2003 – 2009

Position Held:

Residence Counselor

AKA:

Baby Sitter/Nurse/Child Psychologist/Driver/
EMT/Cook/Laundress/Gardener/Community/
Liaison/Nutritionist/Administrative Assistant/Slave

Elapsed Time Before Job Search Resumed:

The search never stopped. Prior to being hired as a full-time paid worker/part-time slave, I was itching to do just about anything else. I was roped into this gig for over four years (a personal record due, in part, to the variety and itinerancy of the slavery and to the amazing economic situation of the 2000s).

Compensation:

$8.75/hour - $10.00/hour

Commute:

An angry drive in The Sex Mobile, listening to the loudest music possible in order to drown out the fact that my life was about to be put completely on hold for twelve-to-thirty-six hours straight. (Author's Note: The Sex Mobile was a fabulous, vintage, white Pontiac Firebird in nearly mint condition. The car of my dreams left over from someone else's high school dream, The Sex Mobile was a random gift from my father. The Sex Mobile, however, got its first dent at Strive House when a neighbor simply backed up into all of its sexiness. Alas.)

Commute Time:

Half hour, each way

Physical Environment:

A house in the 'burbs, devoid of any books, plants, pictures, or much of anything else (save for beds, towels, other people's clothes, and a washer-and-dryer set).

Emotional Environment:

A lot like being held hostage in someone else's home, all the while being forced to watch rap videos and reality TV for hours upon hours while doing never-ending loads of laundry and dishes. All of these tasks were performed in front of an ultra-dysfunctional family only to be administrated at later by one of The Five Horsemen for not having scrubbed the kitchen floor with a toothbrush. (After all, the Board Members/State/contractors were on their way and might notice a crumb near a wastebasket.) No one else in the world lives like this, I swear, unless they have severe obsessive-compulsive disorder.

Nemeses:

The Five Horsemen of the Apocalypse:

Four women, and one man, employed as District Managers. They were hired only for their ability to scare employees into doing more housework. Having some sort of communication disorder and/or a lack of sense of humor was also a pre-requisite for the position. While the entire staff rotated out five times while I was there, none of The Horse People ever left.

The parents:

Who all assumed that their child was the only person with issues living in the house.

The lack of sleep:

It was almost like an endurance experiment to see how long one could keep hold of one's marbles while pretending to remain patient with other human beings (a test I am quite sure I failed every time it was administered).

The State:

While you could make friends with and become comfortable caring for your charges, The State would come in to make sure that everything ran more-than-perfectly. If, by chance, your house and management worked hard to maintain compliance with the myriad rules and regulations, The State would simply change the rules mid-audit, so that the agency would have to return a percentage of its funding. The inspectors were utterly random and they didn't tell anyone the rules of game, so that The State was able to recoup some of its money.

The house, itself:

In my time there, I witnessed the doorbell ringing non-stop when no one was near it, TV, radio and lights that would turn on-and-off by themselves, items that would go missing, things that would fall by themselves.

While I can't cite specific supernatural causes, I can say that it must be very difficult to be disabled for more reasons than meet the eye.

The other counselors:

This was not a job where you wanted to make enemies. (Remember, you have to sleep there after all!)

Allies:

The other counselors

Living Situation(s):

In The Animal House apartment building with my new husband, who seemed relieved that he still had a whole bed to himself at least once each week, but assured me that he missed me anyway.

When I Knew:

When I'd bent over backwards to plan an outing for my developmentally-delayed clients, but ended up with a tick embedded in my gut on said outing, and then got blamed for not being aware that there might be ticks. (I'd spent the bulk of my youth frolicking in woods and hay fields half-naked, and never once, ever, had I garnered my very own tick.) There were also no bathrooms available in the woods or drinks for my charges. (Yet I was supposed to do something absolutely free other than walking them around the mall.) I simply stopped caring about outings and concentrated on the house cleaning and other chores. To The Five Horsemen, this would probably have been deemed totally unacceptable (had they been able to read my mind) as EVERYONE was supposed to care about EVERYTHING *ALL* of The Time. (A physical/mental/emotional impossibility.)

Departure:

This gig was like falling into the La Brea Tar Pits. It was hard to leave, hard to stay, hard to keep, yet they wouldn't let me go.

What I Think About When I Think About This Damn Job:

Waking up during a thunderstorm to find one of my clients staring at me and somehow managing to not scream after I realized where I was. How much I learned, how much I detested it, day after day, year after year, and hated myself for it. How with this particular line of work, if you admit to disliking it, you are suddenly The Devil (yet, everyone says how "special" you are for working with the disabled). I'm not "special." I was simply filling a need. When they didn't need me anymore, they just stopped calling or returning my e-mails. There was nothing "special" about it. How many friends I made in the midst of our collective misery. Watching scores of people come in and leave as soon as they realized how much was really expected of them on a daily basis. How much I hate our health care system.

Weird Bank & Distrust

Employee:

FAXBoy

Location:

Oakland, California

Approximate Tenure:

January 5th, 2003 - March Something 2003

Position Held:

Writer(!)

AKA:

"Lead" Administrative Assistant/Receptionist/Document Formatress/Punching Bag for Communications Beeeeyatch

Elapsed Time Before Job Search Resumed:

A matter of breathless seconds. This just after I was introduced to my "desk" and my phone. The desk was actually just a portion of a long pre-fab unit (much like something you would find in an elementary school lunch room or a German beer garden) that had tiny speed bump partitions that delineated each person's work area. Upon this desk shall NOT be: Any personal items, such as, but not limited to: larger-than-tiny personal photographs, papers (work-related or otherwise), pens, or pretty much anything despite the fact that you were expected to be working constantly on 4,000 separate projects.

Pictures (if you were so bold and so ego-maniacal to bring them in) were to be placed in regulation (and approved, no lie) frames and no other personal effects were (basically) allowed. As for the phone (which I had no idea was to be involved with my "writing" position in any way, shape, or form), no personal calls were to be made (or received) on it. (The phone was only to be picked up when someone internally wanted to rip you a new asshole.) Internet access was essentially limited to the Weird Savings' homepage and there was to be absolutely NO PERSONAL E-MAIL whatsoever. The steno pool was so tightly monitored and restricted in so many ways that I imagined that this must be what rehab (or a women's Federal detention facility) must be like...

Compensation:

$50k/year(!)

Commute:

BART subway, from the Civic Center to the 19th Street station in Oakland, and then three blocks once I resurfaced on the other side of The San Francisco Bay

Commute Time:

20+ minutes each way

Physical Environment:

80s hell. Shiny, onyx office furniture, barrier-less cubes, phone systems and other office machinery from the 1960s.

The building itself was someone's vision of the future years ago that ended up looking like a tricked-out Suburban from the early 90s with its pewter columns, tinted windows, and excessive chrome detailing.

Emotional Environment:

It was like working back at the Regional HMO without the occasional love or what I imagined it must feel like to work in an office in the middle of Iowa. Some of the nastiest bitches on record, EVER, worked at this place.

Nemeses:

Wicked overseer, some nasty-ass manager, named ClaraBelle, who struck me less and less as a biological female the more she smoked and tormented everyone in the typing pool (myself included), Orville Redenfucker -- The bald, dry, dry, dry humored boring Vice President who always tried to correct my grammar, the phone, the raisins who founded this skanky S&L, the everything.

Allies:

Curtissa: My neighbor, my confidant. What a great laugh:-)

Living Situation(s):

Market Street with The Ex-Boyfriend. Special guest appearance by: FileGrrl!

When I Knew:

It had to have been during the orientation when they screened this way-fucked-up safety video about the "ultra modern office tower" that we now so proudly inhabited.

It was made in the late 80s or early 90s, but smacked of the 70s and I couldn't stop laughing at all of the fashions and *Get Smart!* equipment supposedly embedded in the walls. The whole thing read like *Airplane!* meets *The Towering Inferno*. I wish I had a copy, it was that good.

Departure:

Abrupt and shortly after my third or fourth trip to the principal's office where famous phrases such as "Do you even own an iron?" and "Why are you so slow?" were uttered during previous *tête-à-têtes*. Parting shot: "You should probably check your diagnostics because you're the one who hired me." At roughly 11:30PST on a Tuesday morning, I quietly shut down my machine, put on my coat, and caught the next train home while listening to Nirvana's "Scentless Apprentice"(live) over and over again ("*You can't fire me because I quit!*")

What I Think About When I Think About This Damn Job:

The rail yards behind the Port of Oakland, that warehouse full of artists next to the elevated tracks who would hang new work out the window with an e-mail address for critique, the blue tiles in the 19th Street station that looked like they were pried from the walls of an old McDonald's, business names in the area such as: "Oh, My Nappy Hair!" (a salon) and "Gold Teeth Master" (not technically a dentist's office), the coffee and fresh-baked cherry muffins from the Arab cafe on the trail of tears to Weird Savings every morning.

BONUS! Actual Correspondence After the Fact:

From: FAXBoy <FAXBoy@rocketmail.com>

To: FileGrrl <FileGrrl@hotmail.com>

Subject: This Just In From Weird Bank...

Date: Wed, 5 Mar 2003 16:54:54 (PST)

"I just want you to know that there are so many people here who are bummed that you left. Not that we don't completely understand why you left, but we miss you. And poor Curtissa has no one to talk to:-)

Please keep in touch, because I really enjoyed getting to know you, as did a lot of other folks.

What are you going to do? Any chance of being able to go back to your old job?

Best,

Suzy SoAndSo

Corporate Recruiter/Weird Bank & Distrust"

and then:

From: FileGrrl <FileGrrl@hotmail.com>

To: FAXBoy <FAXBoy@rocketmail.com>

Subject: RE: This Just In From Weird Bank...

Date: Wed, 5 Mar 2003 16:54:55 (PST)

Well, Mr. Too Social, your popularity leaves a heartbreaking trail...

MORE INCREDIBLE BONUS ACTION!

Actually saw Orville from the window of the aforementioned café where I wrote this entry (so smug and yet so lame) AND saw ClaraBelle outside of Weird Bank itself SMOKING. More about ClaraHelle: 6'6" (at least), jet black hair cut in a Catholic school style (*mit* barrettes), concave chest, severe (possibly Asian) countenance in a perpetual scowl (except when she attempted to smile, which was terrifying and, thankfully, seldom). Today she was wearing a bright pink Jackie-O number that had the texture of a bath mat that made her look like a C-list drag queen. I think she recognized me. I became invisible and slipped back into the subway...

Bongs N' Schlongs

Employee:

FileGrrl

Location:

Albany, New York

Approximate Tenure:

April 2003- June 2003

Position Held:

Clerk

AKA:

Paranoia Whacker #2

Elapsed Time Before Job Search Resumed:

One week, which was far too long, in retrospect

Compensation:

$7-ish/hour

Commute:

In my beat-up car, or on a bus, and then on foot

Commute Time:

It depended on how I got there. The bus/perambulation combo took an hour, but driving (or getting a ride from anyone who might be going my way) only took 20 minutes

Physical Environment:

Huge, filthy, lavender room that was in the process of being repainted when I got hired. This necessitated moving faux bamboo and wicker furniture from the 70s, and glass cases full of ugly sweaters from Nepal that were covered in dust, the spiders and their nests, and so on and so forth, to roll out the walls. They didn't trust me to paint, so I was given the task of counting the huge selection of glass pipes in the back each and every night. I wasn't part of any sort of drug culture and I didn't know the difference between this pipe, or that pipe, or what the fuck they were called. (These contraptions had also blossomed in form and function since the time when I actually hung out with people who would have known.) The best piece in the store, however, was the shop-worn Jeff Stryker life-cast, still in its battered cardboard box, that had been banished to a dust-laden wicker "sale" basket under a heap of Indian skirts against the wall. I felt bad for ol' Jeff and often wondered what he'd think if he happened to stop by one night to find this facsimile of his spectacular, yet forlorn, manhood relegated to the remainder bin.

Emotional Environment:

This was a classic bait-and-switch job: I saved the newspaper ad for a very long time after the fact to remind myself never to take a job like this ever again. I was hired as a store clerk. I make historical reenactment garments. I love sex. I figured I could combine the best of all worlds and sell my hand-made clothing while displaying my deep product knowledge about the (limited) selection of adult toys and sexual enhancement paraphernalia that they stocked in the store. I've visited large sex boutiques in London, Boston, and San Francisco where I have seen the sales clerks dressed to the nines working in discothèque, party atmospheres with techno blasting through the speakers as they answered any, and every, question a customer might have. Those stores were festive, cordial, informative, engaging, mysterious, and sexy. However, Upstate New York being what it is, I learned that more people get stoned than actually have sex, at least, when it comes to where they spend their money. With so little money actually being spent on lube, vibes, Spanish Fly, rings and the like, the store's owner had long since given up on the sex and had thoroughly embraced their other inventory. (Smart man.)

Since the big sellers were glass pipes and water bongs ("for tobacco use only"), that inventory was kept well stocked. My boss was very business-minded (as only an aging hippie can be) and I was given the nightly task of counting each and every pipe, pipette, bong, tube, stem, screen, hose, and whatchermajig just to curb the paranoia that we were all stealing from him. We were kept frenetic with all the busy-work ("idle hands" and all that...) On slow nights, I also had the option of inventorying all the vibes and odd sexually-related herbal remedies from China.

Nemeses:

The boss's beautiful daughter who had the face of a fairy princess and the demeanor of an ornery stripper. Usually dressed in a plain hoodie and jeans, she'd clearly seen it all in her short life. Her gray eyes were level and cold. She had no interest in humor, excuses, or anyone else. She worked her ass off in the store (as her mother had done) to sell, order, inventory, vacuum, and count out the deposit like clockwork. Sex, in general, was so stale and blasé, that it was no longer a topic up for conversation (if it ever had been). She scared the shit out of me. I only saw her crack once: I'd asked her point blank, "So, was your father in the military, or was he a hippie, or both?" and she looked at me incredulously, laughed, and said, "Both!"

Allies:

The other girls who had worked as store clerks in many other shops. I imagined them secretly working as escorts in their off hours, and one of them actually showed up to her shift with a Vuitton bag "from a man," but my senses told me that she'd recently just attended a *faux* purse party.

Living Situation(s):

With my future husband, a man of tall stature, boring video games, winning Lotto tickets, and long, romantic, rather 18th-century ponytail in The Animal House Arms.

When I Knew:

The first day when I understood the importance of the paraphernalia: I'd really been looking forward to reviewing wholesale catalogs for fancy stockings and clothing imported from India but, instead, I was handed a checklist on a clipboard and a pencil and pointed toward the back wall (which was chock full of nothing I was remotely interested in). I didn't even want to learn anything about it. What am I going to put on a résumé? "Head Bong Counter?" I also knew when a strung-out woman came into the store in the driving rain and asked to look at all the scales we had in stock. She selected the most expensive ($100 - $200 range) and was nearly in tears as she "needed a scale replacement by 4AM." I honestly hope never to be in a position in my life that would require "a scale replacement by 4AM."

I also knew when I went in to get my paycheck and one of the newly hired girls told me that she'd been up all night painting the walls lavender. (I hope they paid her.)

Departure:

Fairly abrupt. I made up an excuse of some sort and ran to a temp agency and simply begged.

What I Think About When I Think About This Damn Job:

The lavender walls. How much I hate the Grateful Dead and Phish. How much I hate the bait-and-switch. How much I hate wasting my time with jobs that can't even be included on a résumé (even though my intentions were good when I took them).

GirlieGlitter.com

Employee:

FAXBoy

Location:

San Francisco, California

Approximate Tenure:

The 2004 Holidaze, from October to January (2005)

Position Held:

Seasonal Employee

AKA:

Telephonic Cannon Fodder

Elapsed Time Before Job Search Resumed:

Already accepted into The Iowa City Skool for Incredibly Famous Writers of The Future, I was looking forward to not working *at all* once I landed in The Midwest

Compensation:

$11-to-15/hour (depending on who you asked, when you asked them, and how they felt at the time that you asked them)

Commute:

Like, ten blocks straight down Market Street

Commute Time: Five minutes in the underground (from Van Ness to the Powell station, *if* the system was open before I had to be "live" on the phones and it wasn't already broken for the day), twenty minutes on foot, or fifteen(-ish) minutes on the beautiful (and historic!) F-Market line. If, however, everything was going my way (like, say, a train) and I got to work vaguely on time, there was *still* Checkpoint Charlie to navigate once I got to the office tower at the corner of Market and First Streets (and this is where I was most likely to lose time if something was going to go wrong on my way to the office).

Once through the revolving doors, I'd race-walk to the front desk where I was always greeted with a generic smile from a revolving cast of generic front-desk personnel who all wore generic blue blazers, white Oxfords, and maroon ties (the women wore some sort of oversized bow or ribbon contraption that all made them look like they were being gored by some unidentifiable, yet bloody and half-dead, rodent). Sometimes my badge wouldn't catch the sensor underneath the black glass embedded in the shiny black marble countertop and the smiles invariably disappeared as the security guard *du jour* instantly put me on both the No-Fly and The Federal Most-Wanted Lists until I took the three steps that I had already taken towards the elevators back to the front desk to walk the technology through the process of verifying my right to enter the building (almost on time). Once cleared for ascension, the elevators asked for the same verification from the same card (via a credit-card slot installed above the bank of numbers for the thirty-seven floors in the building). Often this fucker wouldn't work, either, and I'd stand in an empty elevator by myself with the doors wide open until an employee from another company on another floor would show up and we would wordlessly agree to let my terrorist ass up to the eleventh floor with his/or her valid and functional plastic ID card. As soon as I popped out of said elevator, oven-fresh, I was confronted with a set of locked wooden doors that looked like they had been developed by a strategic partnership between IKEA and BRINKS. I'd swipe my card AGAIN and hope that the stupid light would change from red to green on the first attempt. Safely installed behind three levels of maximum security bullshit, I'd actually step into the dark office, survey the vast cube farm before the start of another useless day, and purposely not turn on the lights (because the all-day fluorescence often made me feel like an old chicken patty under a heat lamp by the end of a shift) in order to enjoy the silence before some of my rowdier co-workers cleared Checkpoint Charlie to fuck up my solitude/poetic introspection.

Physical Environment:

Like the polyamorous lovechild of The Pacific Stock Exchange, a makeup counter at Macy's, and The Publisher's Clearing House call center

Emotional Environment:

Like working at The Pentagon if The U.S. Government were in the market of selling surface-to-air missiles to bored (and drunk) housewives in The Bible Belt, in Hollywood, and on The Upper West Side

Nemeses:

MUNI, the phone, and the glamazons who managed the temps on the front lines

Allies:

Sandra Cisneros (not her real name) and strong, black coffee

Living Situation(s):

The flat on Market Street with The Marijuana Monster, The Marijuana Monster's sister, and The Ex-Boyfriend

When I Knew:

Oh, I knew going into this job that I should never pick up any phone, anywhere, for anyone ever again. However, the rent needed to be paid, so I leased my soul to GirlieGlitter.com through a swanky temp agency.

Departure:

Angry, defensive, and disappointing, but (relatively) official at the end of the assignment.

What I Think About When I Think About This Damn Job:

FUCK! Where to begin? How about "at the beginning"? 'K: Before I walked through the doors at the aforementioned swanky temp agency, I had spent hours (seriously: fucking HOURS) at a shitty temp agency up the street going through their battery of diagnostics. Initially, I was seated at a large blond-wood conference table with a sheaf of forms to fill out by hand. I was surrounded by filing cabinets that looked like old card catalogues from some long-defunct library. The shitty temp agency was run by an angry black dwarf on dialysis (who also had scoliosis or some other malformation of his compact and freakish body) and he had an assistant who, in retrospect, seemed to be trying to signal to me (with the dolorous expression in his eyes and very subtle nods of his head), to run out of the building. (*Now!*) After I finished the paperwork, I was dropped in front of a generic PC to run the Word/Excel/PowerPoint gauntlet in a small storage closet.

After I bashed the keys like a belligerent simian, I ended up face-to-face with the angry dwarf who was angrily reviewing the results of my tests. Despite the fact that I was in my mid-30s at the time, I felt exactly like I had just been dropped in the Principal's office in grade school. The man, tubes emanating from somewhere on his grotesque body, asked me (after exhaling a deep cloud of smelly breath that betrayed him as a heavy smoker), "What do you want to do?" Already fried from jumping through all of the paper- and computer-based hoops, I responded, "Work. Anything. Whatever." And he went off! "With these scores?" he bellowed. After a predictably heated exchange, I told him point-blank, that I hadn't gone to graduate skool "to study Microsoft products." (I know, I know! I *should* have gone to graduate skool to study (fucking) Microsoft products.) Mutually disgusted and pissed off, I scrambled out of the building (off the record: nearly in tears). I looked left up Market Street (and considered just going home) and then looked right and just started walking to the next temp agency. Their lobby, and the demeanor of the all-female staff, made it feel like I had just entered a luxury hotel as a VIP guest. What a difference! It was, of course, all muted smoke and trick mirrors, but at that very moment, it was exactly what I needed (including a job). I filled out more forms, but they were less torturous than the previous stack and went through another battery of Microsoftness, but with the warm-up I had just had, I passed with flying colors! (Or was it simply that I was treated (almost) like a human being? Hmmm… Jury's still out on that one.) The reward for successfully completing this second round of paperwork and diagnostics was another (congratulatory!) stack of paperwork. (Including, "but not limited to," a multi-page confidentiality agreement and several acknowledgements of receipt for the dress code and office etiquette guidelines. All of which were suitable for framing the way that these women were all going on about this assignment.) The big motivational carrot on the end of their big, swanky temp agency stick was a $500 bonus for excellent performance from the very beginning to the bitter end of The Holidaze. I thought, "No problem!" (And, wait for it… I thought wrong!) Training was kinda fun, a lot of role-playing with fellow cannon fodder about the types of calls (and callers) that we could anticipate. Sandra and I were always far too raucous and our scenarios always ended with a clear warning for any potentially high-maintenance, difficult customers: "Bitch, I will *cut* you! I know where you live AND I got your gold card numbers, so DO NOT FUCK WITH ME…" There were reprimands, naturally, but we were excused because of our perceived "enthusiasm." Once we were live, the first few days were almost OK (despite the thirty-seven systems that we had to juggle while simultaneously carrying on a coherent conversation with a complete stranger on the other side of the continent). It got uglier, though, the closer we got to Xmas. Our hours were extended and our lunches cut in half (from 44.5 minutes down to 24.5), but to make this slave-driving more palatable to their temp battalion, they lavished us with stacks of pepperoni pizzas and piles of Buffalo chicken wings (not so great, say, if you happen to be a vegetarian). One day, I was certifiably appalled when one of the glamazon middle managers brought in a

Chipmunks CD that she played at us on a small boom box to "put us in the holiday spirit." I damn near threw that cheap stereo out the window I was so fed up with trying to filter out the high-pitched, computer-manipulated, sing-song voices from the drunk and/or distracted ones on the phone for hours on end. Needless to say, this was infuriating, and not at all festive. People started to crack on the floor, and then drop from the ranks altogether. There was one woman, with whom I trained (briefly) one-on-one, who was the fastest typist I have ever seen (anywhere). She seemed to just wave her hands over the keyboard, like Marie Laveau, to conjure the words on the screen while cooing softly to the woman on the other line like a seasoned 900# operator. I was amazed. And then, somewhere in the thick of the consumer frenzy, she stormed into the (glass-enclosed) big boss's office and proceeded to quit, vehemently, hysterically, and completely in tears. (She. Was. FURIOUS!) I got to watch the whole thing (like on old silent film that's been colorized) as this woman read this other woman the total riot act. It was glorious and triumphant! Glorious and triumphant, that is, until the customer service rep was escorted out of the building by security with her one box clutched tightly to her chest, mascara streaking down her hot cheeks in front of a large captive audience. Other things that I think about when I think about this damn job? Using CNN.com's "Forward This Article to a Friend" feature to lob messages at FileGrrl over the corporate firewall. One particular product training that involved some sort of collagen supplement that I refused to drink (because it was distinctly not vegetarian) and having twenty people staring at me from around a bright-white conference table encouraging me to "just try it" and thinking that this is how the last person to die at Jonestown must have felt. The woman with inoperable cancer who called me from her hospital bed to order truckloads of makeup. The servicewomen who called from Iraq, with bombs bursting in air while they were placing their orders, and the absurdity of all of that. The nastiness of most of the women who called from Texas to inquire, "Where my whorepaint at, pansy?!?"

CAT, Inc.

Employee:

FAXBoy

Location:

Iowa City, Iowa

Approximate Tenure:

The summer of 2005

Position Held:

Professional Essay Scorer

AKA:

Overeducated Head of Cattle

Elapsed Time Before Job Search Resumed:

I didn't so much look for another job but, rather, an escape (like an emergency exit)

Compensation:

Somewhere between $10 and $12/hour

Commute:

I either took the North Dodge bus from The Old Crapitol Mall, hitched a ride with a fellow herdsman (or woman), or just hoofed it

Commute Time:

On the bus it could take, like, 20 minutes, in a car it only took four and-a-half minutes, but on foot I could lose over an hour of my life

Physical Environment:

A huge corrugated aluminum warehouse full of buffet tables and folding chairs. (You know, the kind of structure that tornadoes love to shred in The Midwest.)

Emotional Environment:

Like a penal colony for artists and writers

Nemeses:

All of the nearly-illiterate children who wrote the essays that we had to read and evaluate for eight hours a day. The corporate trainers from College Aptitude Testing, Inc. who spoke to us as if we were, in fact, the nearly-illiterate children who wrote said atrocious essays (even though most of us had at least one Master's degree and some members of the herd had multiple PhDs). The beautiful summer sun that surrounded the warehouse, but was never allowed in.

Allies:

Any of the artists and/or writers in the herd that I could skip work with

Living Situation(s):

In a tiny one-bedroom apartment with The Ex-Boyfriend and a very fat cat

When I Knew:

When the corporate trainer (with the flaccid little ponytail stuck to the back of his head) suggested that, "Perhaps, [you aren't] the best person to score these tests," when I told him that the essay that he was holding up as exemplary was one of the worst things that I had ever read in my entire life. (I actually blurted, "Are you fucking kidding me?!?" to the cattle seated around me.)

Departure:

I was released back into the wild with the others at the end of the project (and we were more than happy to leave, every single last one of us).

What I Think About When I Think About This Damn Job:

The big green dinosaur with the creepy smile in front of the Sinclair gas station at top of the road that led down to the warehouse from Dodge Street. (Maybe he, or she, was supposed to be an anthropomorphized brontosaurus, but why the hell was he/or she so happy about the fact that all of his/or her friends and family had already been converted into petroleum products?) The cool Pakistani guy who worked (morning, noon, and night/nine days a week) behind the counter, the awful coffee that he made, and the slew of Iowa-themed gifts that lined his dusty shelves (lighters, shot glasses, commemorative spoons, and anything with an ear of corn printed on it that was invariably manufactured in China). The tiny, wood-paneled break room and the daily battle royale for the dirty microwaves while hundreds of temps went on their 28.5-minute lunch hours simultaneously. An essay from a very precocious teenager that started a little something like this:

"Dear Essay Scorer,

You're a tool and I hate you.

I don't want to be taking this test right now and you've fucked up your life (so majorly!) that you've been forced to read my shitty writing today just to pay the rent on your overpriced apartment this month…"

It went on from there, but it hammered home the fact that everyone else in the cavernous space with me had also majored in something completely useless (not a computer science geek among us). Sitting next to a poet for a few days before she left for a literary festival in Prague and feeling a little Ben Affleck to her Matt Damon. Thinking that everything would be fine once I started workshops at The Iowa City Skool for Incredibly Famous Writers of The Future in the fall.

Nurses, Etc.

Employee:

FileGrrl

Location:

Troy, New York

Approximate Tenure:

Four weeks in the spring of 2010

Position Held:

Medical Biller

AKA:

FileGrrl

Elapsed Time Before Job Search Resumed:

Four weeks

Compensation:

$11.00/hour

Commute:

A drive back to a city that I used to live in. (Where was this job when I lived there?)

Commute Time:

Half-an-hour (made slightly shorter by Metallica)

Physical Environment:

An antique building on The Hudson River with its very own early 20th-century parking garage

Emotional Environment: Slightly annoying. The job itself soon revealed its true nature: A series of if/then statements a mile long from which there could be no deviation. Every (each and every) time I came back into the room I heard, "FileGrrl, you skipped this 999 code." "FileGrrl, you didn't add the right number here." "FileGrrl, put the number above the name of the doctor, not below it." "FileGrrl, you didn't use the correct team code." I was trying, even: I went to bed early. I packed nutritious lunches and wore a watch so I could track my break times. I showered and brushed my teeth so that I was not hygienically offensive. I wore clean clothes and tried to stick to bland, matching outfits that declared nothing whatsoever about my actual personality. I arrived fifteen minutes early and I tried to never talk about myself, ever. I punched in numbers all day and tried to act polite. I cribbed everyone's name on a piece of paper to help me remember who they all were. I was doing my damnedest, but man, they were balls-out difficult! Obviously, I was once again forced to do something that I wasn't particularly good at. If my mind drifted away to think of, say, Egypt, or food, or world history, or WhenTheFuckDoIGetToGoHome for one split second, I made an irretrievable data entry error that would force me to stop, tell on myself, and then have someone fix it in the system. It was vastly humiliating.

Nemeses:

The data entry itself

Allies:

The nurses, who worked very hard at their nearly impossible jobs that involved pleasing insurance companies and clients and doctors all at once. (Note that insurance companies come before clients and doctors.) They frequently vented about how stupid everything was, they played by the rules and followed best practices, they gave 110% each day. I loved them. Fast-talkin' Jean, in particular.

Living Situation(s):

With my husband and three cats in third-floor walk-up apartment, the financial and physical catastrophe of which is not entirely lost on me.

When I Knew:

When the agency called and told me not to go to work as Nurses, Etc. had run out of funding for the position. I thought, "Oh, darn." This one was a fast-paced, ludicrous, important, sweet job that I actually really liked (save for the enforcement of some imported office rules from Toyota – see below). I even liked the sarcastic girl who sat next to me and talked way too fast. I liked the data entry because it was always different and always important and always very tricky.

Departure:

Abrupt. (Well, it wouldn't be the first time.) I stayed home and cleaned the kitchen. Or perhaps I splurged and saw two movies back-to-back. Jobs ended so frequently that I have a hard time remembering which sudden days of freedom belonged to which sudden freedom activities.

What I Think About When I Think About This Damn Job: The other temps and their infamous departures. I'd been temping for so long that I could recognize the remnants of the Ones Who Came Before right away: The still-pristine rule books, issued but never read, the notes about how to perform the job's tasks, the wayward fake Tupperware® full of *something*. I asked Jean what had been wrong with all the previous temps and got an earful: One said point blank to her trainer, "Don't confuse yourself." *What?* Her trainer's response was a curt, "I do not confuse myself." The poor temp had no clue that as a temp, you are The Office Moron until proven otherwise. (This initiation period usually lasts from one-to-three months, depending on the office.) One temp took all the papers she needed to perform her job home with her and apparently never returned. *Why would you take any information home?* Data entry isn't like an exam that you need to study for! You just key in what they tell you -- You either do it well, or you don't. The temp just prior to me did the opposite. She left behind the stuff she was *supposed* to take home and read: The never-ending HIPPA regulations, personal conduct rules, ethics, and on and on. I found it all buried beneath the pile of task outlines that I used to do my own work.

Upon presentation with same, I took all of my rules home and dutifully recycled them. I've read them so often that I could write them. One temp told Jean that she wasn't going to have hair the next day and then lifted her wig to show off her bald pate, already shaved. Jean thought the gesture mortifyingly inappropriate for work. I thought it was funny and dumb, but I chose to keep my own hair (for the duration of the gig, at least). The day that my trainer walked into the room with a gaggle of nurses: I thought she was plowing her way to her desk and needed to ask her a question. She was not, however, as available as she looked. She was "in a meeting" and snipped, "Could you wait until I'm not in a meeting?" The group standing behind my desk one day was the "LEAN Team," an ergonomic/work production crew originally created by Toyota which, as they say, was like Socialism: great on paper. *Eliminate work-flow redundancy? Sign me up!* Either by brilliant design, or through over-exuberance, LEAN forces people to work with the bare minimum at their desks, with each stapler not only labeled, but the space for each office supply on the desk also labeled. Thus, the paper clips are labeled, and in turn, their spot on the desk is labeled, etc., and so on, and so forth. I suppose it was developed to rein in cube workers who are inclined to decorate their workspaces with wrapping paper, disco balls, and live gold fish, but it really is a whole new level of forced minimalism (and a whole new level of dumb-ass). Whenever "LEAN" was mentioned, I kept choking back my escaped snorts lest they turn into unstoppable peals of laughter. My desk mate had an "LEAN Team" certificate hung proudly over her/our shared desk, tacked to her bulletin board full of cats/children/man pictures. All pictures themselves, according to "LEAN Team" standards, must be mounted according to personal/work divisions. Work-related information may be posted on one board; any personal information on its own, separate board. Nothing is supposed to escape from the bulletin boards on to the actual wall or your team/department gets demerits. This type of micro-management makes it all too easy, and tempting, to stage rebellion. I tacked all sorts of shit to the wall just above my phone, like things that were missing to actually perform my job (for example, the list of phone extensions for the nurses in my office). *WTF? Thanks, Toyota!* I also think of the river and of freedom, or freedom and then the river, depending on the day.

The Smalltown Dark-Times

Employee:

FileGrrl

Location:

Albany, New York

Approximate Tenure:

Two weeks during the winter of 2010

Position Held:

Newspaper Carrier

AKA:

Lost

Elapsed Time Before Job Search Resumed:

Ongoing -- I've never really stopped searching for gainful employment

Compensation:

$150 - $156/week, minus coffee and frequent pit stops

Commute:

Most of the commute for this gig happened at 3AM in my bedroom where I tried every day to wake up before my husband hit the snooze button for the second time in order to avoid coma and early termination. Then I'd toss on yesterday's clothes, left in reverse order of appearance on the floor (and god forbid gremlins broke in to rearrange them while I was not paying attention or my bra might end up on my head, or worse). Next, I'd exit the apartment building into a morning still strewn with last night's revelers as they crawled home after last call in their chic boots and scarves, clinging to each other for physical support from that last, unnecessary pint or Cosmo. The cold air would sting my eyes, and I'd be a little jealous of the children dragging themselves into the new day, but I was also (usually) secretly relieved that I'd made it through that particular portion of my life relatively unscathed.

Commute Time:

Ten minutes for what should really be a twenty-minute endeavor

Physical Environment: Total Borg Collective: The newspaper (in general) is dying and they knew it. Because of print's imminent demise, subscription rates had toppled and, while at least 100+ Borg labor away in the early morning to get the news to the people of the land, the word of the day was that we should enjoy the work while we had it, because it wouldn't be long now. The work itself was physically and emotionally demanding in ways that defied the common notion of the neighborhood kid happily tossing papers from his bike to porches along his route. Because of this, people were dropping out of this job like flies off a dirty ceiling. We each had workstations (rented for $1/week, presumably to help the paper offset the rent of the warehouse). Each workstation had the name of the last soul to occupy the space and to service that route, but people came and went so quickly that the managers had stopped adding people's names to these stations. Most of us were numbers. I was 14.

Emotional Environment:

With the exception of a kind-hearted supervisor, who also roused himself out of bed somewhere between 2 and 3AM, the level of dehumanization in this huge warehouse was astounding. I greeted my workstation neighbors cheerfully as "43" and "13." I felt waves of pity for everyone in the room, from the top down. I wished I had 12 clones to lift the burden that these news carriers have: 175 or more newspapers hand-delivered to people who all get up during the same two-hour window.

Nemeses:

Time and the weather. If I was too late (and I was late every day), then subscribers called to complain. After the sun came up, and other drivers hit the road, delivery became hazardous and slowed me down even further. If it was snowing, my feet got wet and cold (I purchased new, cheap boots with my first tiny paycheck), the driveways became impassable, and I had to be more careful about tossing the papers so they didn't land bag-open in the snow like birds that had been filleted mid-air. One of my friends from high school was decapitated while delivering papers from her car one bright morning in the mid-80s. I'd always wondered how she had died on her own street going no more than a few miles an hour and I never stopped thinking about her head, or mine, when the sun came up every morning.

Allies:

This was the kindest crew I'd ever worked with (or for). It was some sort of brotherhood of misery. Every one of them got up at 3AM and they were supportive and helpful in ways I never could have predicted or imagined.

Living Situation(s):

A student apartment with my husband and three sleep-deprived, confused cats.

When I Knew:

When, after delivering one-hundred and seventy-five papers in the wee hours of a freezing and humorless Sunday morning, I realized it was my job to go back to the depot and bag up another two hundred, as the paper, in its desperation for subscribers, was rallying the delivery crew to obtain new and former subscribers on our route. My car had gone through $50 in gas, the "Check All 'Yer Damn Gauges" light came on for the third time that week, my apartment was a wreck, and I smelled vaguely like a homeless person as I lived in my car for five-to-six hours a day. By 10AM, my papers were all delivered, I was ready for a cup of coffee, a shower and breakfast, yet it would take me several more hours of work to obtain those new required subscribers. I hit an emotional wall, called my boss, and told him I was done.

Departure:

Abrupt. I knew that if I didn't get the car looked at, I wouldn't have one. Although I knew I wouldn't have minded newspaper delivery as a regular hourly job, getting up at 3AM every day with *no day off* was altering my personality in unforeseen ways: I was depressed, nearly suicidal, and totally dysfunctional in a very short period of time. I learned important things about myself during this job -- Namely that I care too much about people to simply leave their papers at the bottom of their drives in the snow and rain and that this fact hampered any future I might have had as a fringe newspaper deliverer.

And that I care too much about myself to get up at 3AM every single day because, even in my admittedly disordered life, some vague biorhythm still exists.

What I Think About When I Think About This Damn Job:

Charles Bukowski. Snow. How *ugly* and unnecessary most people's landscaping really is. The difficulty of finding 17 Wherever Place in the pitch dark (at least firemen have a fighting chance, something is on fire and presumably illuminating the scene for them). How taking care of one's physical self, even in the smallest of ways, improves life exponentially. How much the cold doesn't bother me much once I'm running. How there might not really be any job for me at this late date. How gorgeous the sky is at dawn.

FIN

Acknowledgements

FAXBoy and FileGrrl are indebted to George W. Bush, without whose random and inadvertent support for the arts this book might never have been completed:

Department of the Treasury
Internal Revenue Service
Notice 1377 (February 2008)
Catalog Number 51255B
www.irs.gov

Economic Stimulus Payment Notice

Dear Taxpayer:

We are pleased to inform you that the United States Congress passed and President George W. Bush signed into law the Economic Stimulus Act of 2008, which provides for economic stimulus payments to be made to over 130 million American households. Under this new law, you may be entitled to a payment of up to $600 ($1,200 if filing a joint return), plus additional amounts for each qualifying child.

We are sending this notice to let you know that based on this new law the IRS will begin sending the one-time payments starting in May. To receive a payment in 2008, individuals who qualify will not have to do anything more than file a 2007 tax return. The IRS will determine eligibility, figure the amount, and send the payment. This payment should not be confused with any 2007 income tax refund that is owed to you by the federal government. Income tax refunds for 2007 will be made separately from this one-time payment.

For individuals who normally do not have to file a tax return, the new law provides for payments to individuals who have a total of $3,000 or more in earned income, Social Security benefits, and/or certain veterans' payments. Those individuals should file a tax return for 2007 to receive a payment in 2008.

Individuals who qualify may receive as much as $600 ($1,200 if married filing jointly). Even if you pay no income tax but have a total of $3,000 or more in earned income, Social Security benefits, and/or certain veterans' payments, you may receive a payment of $300 ($600 if married filing jointly).

In addition, individuals eligible for payments may also receive an additional amount of $300 for each child qualifying for the child tax credit.

For taxpayers with adjusted gross income (AGI) of more than $75,000 (or more than $150,000 if married filing jointly), the payment will be reduced or phased out completely.

To qualify for the payment, an individual, spouse, and any qualifying child must have a valid Social Security number. In addition, individuals cannot receive a payment if they can be claimed as a dependent of another taxpayer or they filed a 2007 Form 1040NR, 1040NR-EZ, 1040-PR, or 1040-SS.

All individuals receiving payments will receive a notice and additional information shortly before the payment is made. In the meantime, for additional information, please visit the IRS website at www.irs.gov.

Author Bios

Author and Disemployment Specialist, FAXBoy holds an MFA from The Iowa City Skool for Incredibly Famous Writers of The Future. (**FAXBoy@rocketmail.com**)

Author and Disemployment Specialist, FileGrrl holds a BA in Fine Art and has just completed an MA in Something More Marketable. Her rock journalism, poetry, and nonfiction have appeared in publications and Web journals such as *Buzz Magazine*, *Salvage*, and *The Hidden City*. FileGrrl's visual work has also appeared in galleries throughout the great State of New York.
(**FileGrrl@hotmail.com**)

Made in the USA
Monee, IL
10 June 2023

35475095R00125